MATT CHRISTOPHER

On the Course with...

Tiger Woods

MATT CHRISTOPHER

On the Course with...

Tiger Woods

Text by Glenn Stout

Little, Brown and Company

Boston   New York   London

First Edition

Matt Christopher™ is a trademark of Catherine M. Christopher.

Cover photograph by Anthony Neste

Library of Congress Cataloging-in-Publication Data

Stout, Glenn.
    On the course with—Tiger Woods / Glenn Stout.
      p.   cm.
    Summary: Discusses the personal background and golf career of the popular young golfer who won the Masters Tournament in 1997.
    ISBN 0-316-13445-7
    1. Woods, Tiger—Juvenile literature.   2. Golfers—United States—Biography—Juvenile literature.   3. Racially mixed people—United States—Biography—Juvenile literature.   [1. Woods, Tiger.
2. Golfers.   3. Racially mixed people—Biography.]   I. Title.
GV964.W66C57   1998
796.352'092—dc21
[B]   97-36990

10 9 8 7 6

COM-MO

Printed in the United States of America

Contents

MATT CHRISTOPHER

On the Course with...
Tiger Woods

Prologue

The New Master

As Tiger Woods walked from the practice putting green to the first tee before beginning his final round in the 1997 Masters Tournament in Augusta, Georgia, a tall, athletically built, middle-aged African-American man approached him.

Tiger stopped and warmly greeted former professional Lee Elder, one of the few African-Americans to play pro golf before Tiger Woods.

Elder was a pioneer. When he was young, African-Americans weren't allowed to play professional golf against whites. Elder never even played golf until he was sixteen, when he learned by sneaking onto all-white courses at dusk, after the other golfers had left. In the mid-1960s he became the first African-American to enjoy success on the Professional Golf Association (PGA) tour.

Elder spent much of his career stalking the Masters, one of professional golf's so-called major championships, a list that also includes the British Open, U.S. Open, and Professional Golf Association Championship. In order to play in the Masters, a golfer must win one of a number of qualifying tournaments. For years, Elder never won a qualifying tournament, although on several occasions he just missed doing so.

But Elder was drawn to the tournament by more than its prestige. For years, the Augusta National Club, a private club that operated the course, had no African-American members. The Masters Tournament's founder, Clifford Robinson, was once quoted as saying, "As long as I'm alive, golfers will be white and the caddies will be black." So it was not until 1975, when Lee Elder finally qualified for the Masters by winning the Monsanto Open, that an African-American ever played on the course at all.

In fact, the Augusta National Club did not recruit an African-American member until 1991. As of the spring of 1997, only two African-Americans belonged. Even during the Masters, the only time all year the course is open to spectators, African-American faces in the crowd are rare.

But this year's Masters was different. On this day, among the thousands of white, mostly older male fans, were African-Americans, young people, and women. Looking over the assembled multitude, one had the sense that one was looking at a sampler of American life. Everyone was represented.

The reason for the change was twenty-one-year-old golf phenomenon Tiger Woods. Tiger had earned an invitation to play at Augusta following each of his victories in the U.S. Amateur. He had a real chance to win, and his fans in the crowd were there to see it happen.

Elder whispered a few private words of encouragement to Woods, then sent him on his way with a gentle pat on the shoulder.

Woods knew what his appearance in the tournament meant to people like Elder, and paused for a moment to reflect on the path that had brought him to Augusta. Then, walking through the large crowd that stretched as far as the eye could see around the first hole, he stepped onto the tee and pushed those thoughts from his mind.

This was a golf tournament, and it was time to play. He now thought only about winning and what it would take for him to do so. His next shot, the next hole, the next round, were all that mattered now. If he played to the best of his ability, there would be plenty of time after the tournament to reflect more on what his presence at Augusta could mean.

He carefully placed the ball on the tee, and stood alongside it, placing his feet and body in the proper position. He wiggled the club back and forth a few times and concentrated on what he wanted to do.

Then suddenly, almost without warning, Woods drew the club back, twisting his shoulders so his back faced the course, until the club's shaft was nearly parallel to the ground.

He paused for a millisecond, then uncoiled. He twisted his shoulders back around and swung the club down and through, driving the ball in an explosive blur, his hips flying open and the momentum of his swing twisting his upper body a full 180 degrees.

The club made a *whoosh*ing noise through the air, then a faint solid tick as it struck the ball at nearly 180 miles per hour, faster and more powerfully than the stroke of any other golfer on the professional tour.

Tiger absolutely crushed it. The ball soared through the air, landed in the middle of the fairway more than three hundred yards away, then bounced and rolled thirty or forty yards more. The crowd burst into unchecked cheers and applause.

Tiger Woods had come a long way in twenty-one years. Over the next few hours, he would discover just how much farther he could go.

If you've never played before, golf may look complicated. Actually, it is very simple to understand. Golf is usually played on a large grassy course that consists of eighteen different holes. The object of the game is to hit the golf ball into a four-inch-diameter hole with as few swings, or strokes, of the golf club as possible.

The game of golf can be traced back several thousand years. The ancient Romans played a primitive form of the sport called *paganica,* hitting a leather ball filled with feathers with a bent stick. In Scotland in the mid-1700s, the game took on its modern form. The first golf courses in the United States were built in the 1880s.

The golfer starts each hole at the tee, or beginning of the hole. The ball is placed on a small peg, also called a "tee." The first shot is called a "drive" or "tee shot." The grass-covered expanse between the tee and the hole is called "the fairway." The fairway is often bordered by trees, streams, ponds, hummocks of earth called "bunkers," or long grass called "the rough." Golfers want to stay away from these areas.

A golfer carries many clubs to hit the ball. Clubs come in various lengths, and the head of each is angled differently so the golfer can hit the ball in different ways. After the first shot, a golfer changes clubs frequently to hit successive shots of shorter lengths until he or she reaches the green.

The green is a small area where the grass is cut very short. It is usually surrounded by bunkers or "sand traps," small pits filled with sand. If a ball lands in a sand trap, it is very difficult to hit it out.

Once the golfer hits the ball onto the green, he or she taps the ball to make it roll into the cup. This is called a "putt."

After the putt lands the ball in the hole, the number of strokes it took to make the shot is counted. Each golf course establishes how many strokes a good score for each hole is. This is called "par." Most holes are 150 to 550 yards from tee to green, with par being three, four, or five strokes.

If a golfer reaches the hole in one shot fewer than par — that is, on a par-4 hole, the shot is made in three strokes — it is called a "birdie." Two shots under is an "eagle." Three shots under is an "albatross." One shot over par is a "bogey."

Most courses have eighteen holes. The sum total par for courses usually ranges from 70 to 72, so a golfer who shoots near these numbers is considered a very good player. Yet of the millions of people who play golf, only a very few can consistently shoot a par score. For most players, a score of 90 or less is considered good.

But the very best players might shoot in the 60s. If a player is that good, he or she may have the opportunity to play professionally. Professional golfers play in big tournaments against one another. The winner of a single tournament may earn as much as half a million dollars.

Today, Tiger Woods is the youngest, most exciting, and most talented player in professional golf. At an age when most of his friends are still in college, he is playing golf against the best players in the world.

How did he become so good while so young? Well, an early start helped.

Chapter One:
1975–1976

The Son

One afternoon in the summer of 1976, in the garage of his home in Cypress, California, Earl Woods carefully placed a golf ball on an old worn piece of carpet, and stood over the ball with a club in his hands. A few yards away hung a large, rectangular net.

Woods placed the club head behind the ball and took careful aim. Then he slowly lifted the club back, coiled it around his head, and swung.

Thwock! The sound of the club striking the ball was a sound Earl found satisfying. The ball rocketed into the net and fell harmlessly to the floor.

A tiny voice gurgled with delight.

Earl turned, smiling, and looked at his six-month-old son. Eldrick Woods sat in his high chair, eyes glued to his father. There was nothing the young boy seemed to enjoy more than watching his father hit a golf ball. Eldrick's mother, Kultida, even had a difficult time getting Eldrick to eat when Earl was hitting golf balls. He was content to sit and watch for hours.

Earl enjoyed spending time with the baby. He had three other children from an earlier marriage, but that marriage had failed while Earl pursued a career in the United States Army. He was a good father even then, but the demands of his career had taken him from his family for extended periods of time. When Eldrick was born, he promised himself he would spend as much time as possible with his new son.

Earl Woods's own parents hadn't spent much time with him while he was growing up. He was born in Manhattan, Kansas. His father was African-American and his mother both African-American and Cherokee, a Native American Indian tribe. They were one of only a few African-American families in town.

When Earl Woods was only thirteen, his father died. His mother passed away shortly after that, and Earl was forced to grow up fast.

Despite his misfortune, Earl stayed in school and studied hard. He was an excellent student and a star baseball player on his high school team. After graduation, he enrolled in Kansas State University.

Standing well over six feet tall and weighing more than two hundred pounds, Earl made the college baseball team as a catcher. He was the first African-American to play baseball in the Big Seven (now Big Eight) conference.

Although his teammates accepted him, when the team traveled to road games Earl often had trouble. Just because he was African-American, sometimes he wasn't allowed to eat in the same restaurants as his teammates or stay in the same hotels.

But Earl didn't get discouraged or quit the team. He knew that getting angry wasn't going to help the situation. Instead, he let his powerful bat and throwing arm do the talking for him.

After graduation, Earl joined the United States Army. He married his girlfriend Barbara, and the couple soon had three children: two sons, named Earl Jr. and Kevin, and a daughter, Royce.

Earl Woods was made for the army. His self-discipline and intelligence allowed him to advance quickly in the ranks. He soon settled into a desk job in Brooklyn, New York, as an army information officer.

In this job, Earl did public relations work for the army, writing press releases and handling requests from the media. He was good at his job and probably could have remained in the position until he retired.

But after nearly ten years in the military, Woods became disillusioned. Sitting behind a desk wasn't very challenging anymore.

He decided to apply to the Green Berets, one of the army's elite combat units. Admission and training standards are tough. Green Berets have to be strong both physically and mentally. Once in combat, they usually handle the most dangerous assignments. Very few soldiers who apply to become Green Berets successfully complete the training program.

But Earl Woods was a survivor. Growing up alone had made him strong inside, and he was still physically fit. He thrived under the intense training the Berets received and made the unit as an explosives expert.

Yet even this achievement did not satisfy Earl Woods. He wanted a challenge. He volunteered for combat.

In the mid-1960s, the United States was fighting a war in Southeast Asia, assisting South Vietnam in their struggle against North Vietnam.

The war was fought in unique conditions. The North Vietnamese were masters of jungle warfare and surprise attacks known as "guerrilla warfare." Earl Woods's unit adopted the tactics of their enemy. He often went on patrol deep into enemy territory with small groups of soldiers. They had to be on guard every second of every day.

Even among the Green Berets, Woods was a leader, reaching the rank of lieutenant colonel. After his tour of duty ended, he could have returned to the United States and spent the remainder of the war training other soldiers. But Woods thrived in pressure situations. He volunteered for combat a second time.

While on his second tour of duty, Woods was assigned to a unit made up of both American and South Vietnamese soldiers. His South Vietnamese counterpart was a soldier named Nguyen Phong.

Woods and Nguyen Phong made an unlikely pair. Woods was a big man, and African-American, while

Phong was slight in stature and Vietnamese. But their differences meant little to each other. Working side by side, they became close friends.

Woods admired Phong, and considered him the best soldier he ever served with. He nicknamed him "Tiger," because of his bravery and the stealthy way he moved through the jungle. On several occasions during combat, Phong's quick thinking saved Earl Woods's life.

Despite their closeness, after Woods's second tour of duty ended, he lost track of his friend. But he never forgot the man he called "Tiger."

When Earl returned to the United States, he made a difficult decision. The long separation from his family while he was in Vietnam had taken a toll on his marriage. He and Barbara divorced, and once again Woods set off for duty overseas. This time he was sent to Thailand.

While there he met a beautiful young half-Thai, half-Chinese secretary who worked in a military office. He asked the woman, Kultida, out on a date. Before too long, the two were in love.

When his assignment in Thailand ended, he asked Tida to return to the United States and marry him.

She agreed, and soon after they returned to the United States in 1969, the two were married.

Woods was again stationed in Brooklyn. He remained in the army for the next five years. Then, in the year before he planned to retire, Earl took up golf.

For months, a fellow army officer had been urging him to give the game a try. Earl finally agreed, and the two men went to the base's golf course.

Woods thought the game would be easy for him. After all, he had been good at baseball, a game in which the ball moved before it was hit. He thought that hitting a little golf ball sitting stationary on the ground would be easy.

It wasn't. He struggled to make solid contact with the ball and send it in the direction he wanted. In the first round of golf he ever played, Earl lost badly.

After the defeat, Woods vowed to himself that before he retired, he would beat his friend. For the next several months, he spent all his spare time at the base driving range, practicing his stroke by hitting bucket after bucket of balls.

The game didn't come to him easily. When he was growing up, golf was a game played by wealthy white people at private clubs that cost hundreds and even thousands of dollars to join. Despite his reputation as a fine athlete, Earl never had the opportunity to play as a child. As he told a reporter years later, "I was a black kid and golf was played at the country club. End of story."

Now Earl was determined to make up for lost time. Several months after their first match, Woods challenged his friend to another game.

His hours of practice paid off. Earl shot an 81, a good score for an amateur player, and beat his friend by four shots. From that moment on, he was hooked on golf.

Earl retired from the army and he and Tida moved to California. Woods took a job with McDonnell Douglas, a company that makes military equipment.

Shortly after they arrived in California, Tida became pregnant. The couple decided to buy a house.

They selected a home in Cypress, California, just a few minutes' drive from Earl's workplace. There was a park nearby and the elementary school was only two blocks away. They decided it would be the perfect place to raise their child.

Earl Woods knew that there were no other African-American or Asian families in the neighborhood, but that didn't bother him. He had always gotten along with everyone.

While most of their neighbors welcomed Earl and Kultida to the neighborhood, others did not. Some neighborhood teenagers harassed the couple, shooting BB-guns at their windows and throwing limes at their house. They hoped to frighten the Woodses into moving away.

But Earl was not easily intimidated. After all, he had been a Green Beret. Once the teenagers realized Earl wasn't afraid, the harassment stopped.

Now, for the first time in his life, he had time to relax and enjoy life. Even though he had a job, he had plenty of time to do what he wanted. He set up a makeshift driving range in the garage and kept working on his golf game.

Although Earl knew he was too old to learn to play well enough to be a professional, he was still determined to master the game. He practiced as many shots as possible in his garage, and then played on local public courses.

He allowed himself only one distraction — his son.

Eldrick Woods was born on December 30, 1975. His mother named him by combining letters from the first names of both her and her husband. But Earl Woods never called his son Eldrick. He called him "Tiger," in honor of his old friend Nguyen Phong. Earl hoped his son would grow up to have some of the same qualities he had admired in Phong.

True to his promise, Earl spent as much time as possible with his baby son. When he saw how much little Tiger enjoyed watching him practice golf, he took an old golf putter, a club used to putt the ball, cut off most of the handle, and gave it to the boy. Someday, thought Earl, I'll teach him how to play.

But one day when Tiger was only nine months old and barely walking, something remarkable happened. As Earl sat down and rested after striking hundreds of balls, he watched Tiger wiggle out of his high chair, pick up his little club, and toddle over to the piece of carpet. Tiger picked up a stray ball, placed it in front of him, looked at the netting, looked back down at the ball, then coiled the club behind his head like his father and swung.

Thwock! The ball rocketed into the net. Tiger Woods giggled.

Earl Woods was so surprised he almost fell out of his chair. The boy's swing was perfect, like a diagram in an instructional book about golf. Earl raced into the house and shouted to Tida, "We've got a genius on our hands!"

The remarkable career of Tiger Woods had just begun.

Chapter Two:
1976–1981

The Prodigy

As much as Tiger's precocious ability to hit a golf ball excited Earl, it also worried him. He wanted to encourage Tiger to play, but knew he had to be careful or he might inadvertently scare him away from golf. After all, Tiger was just a baby.

Earl promised himself that he would never force the game on his son. If Tiger wanted to play, Earl would be pleased, but if he didn't, Earl wasn't going to push him.

At first, Earl didn't even try to give Tiger any help. He just let him hit the ball into the net and watched to see if he would remain interested.

Tiger loved it. To him, golf wasn't a game or a sport. Tiger was too young even to know what those were. All he knew was that it was fun to hit the ball.

In the beginning, Tiger swung left-handed, and was actually hitting balls with the back of his little putter. But after a few weeks, all on his own, he turned around and started swinging right-handed.

The change convinced Earl more than ever that Tiger was born to play the game. Ever so slowly, he started teaching Tiger about golf.

For someone new to the game, one of the most confusing things about golf is the large number of clubs used. Each player has about a dozen clubs, and each is different. Clubs called "woods" are long, and their wide, heavy club heads are mounted nearly perpendicular to the ground, so a golfer can hit long, low shots. Clubs called "irons" are shorter, and the club head is flat and angled so a golfer can hit the ball a shorter distance but higher in the air and with more accuracy. Both woods and irons are numbered. The higher the number, the shorter the club.

Other clubs called "wedges" are used to loft or "pitch" the ball softly into the air or dig it out from the rough or a sand trap. On the green, the golfer uses a putter, a short club with a wide, flat face, to roll the ball.

Because every hole is different, every shot is different. A golfer must learn how to use each club. It can take many years to learn how to play the game well.

Yet it took Tiger only a few years to begin to play as well as most adults. At the age of eighteen months, Earl started taking him to the driving range. He cut down several other clubs for the boy, so Tiger could practice with each and learn how they differed from one another.

Tiger behaved as if he had been born on the driving range. When other golfers saw the toddler practicing, they laughed. But soon their laughter changed to stares of amazement as the little boy hit ball after ball straight and true.

Earl then decided to try an experiment. He snuck Tiger onto the navy golf course where he often played and allowed him to play a hole. From the tee to the green it was 410 yards, a par 4, meaning a very good golfer should get the ball in the hole in four shots.

At the tee, Earl set the ball up for Tiger and watched. Tiger swung, and the ball sailed down the middle of the fairway. He didn't hit the ball far, but he hit it straight.

The only concession Earl made for the boy was to place the ball on a tee before each shot, not just the first one. Tiger simply wasn't strong enough to get the ball off the ground if it was buried in the grass.

It took Tiger seven more shots to reach the green. Once on the smooth grass surface, the little boy made the hole in only three putts, to score an eleven.

Earl was impressed. When he first began playing the game, he hadn't done much better. But Earl was a grown man. Tiger wasn't even three feet tall. He still wore diapers and drank milk from a bottle.

Now Earl began teaching Tiger in earnest. Tiger was starting to talk and ask questions. Before long, he and his father were having long, complicated conversations about the mechanics of a golf swing and golfing strategy. Earl continued bringing the boy onto the golf course to practice. Each time he did, Tiger improved.

Earl and Kultida were proud. When Tiger turned two years old, his mother called up a Los Angeles television station and told a reporter, former pro football player Jim Hill, that her two-year-old son could play golf. Although Hill was skeptical, Kultida

Woods was convincing. Hill agreed to come out with a camera crew to watch Tiger play.

They met on a golf course and Hill and his crew watched as Tiger expertly played the hole.

Tiger didn't look like a little boy playing golf. He looked like a miniature adult. His swing was technically perfect, and he knew exactly what he was doing on each shot. The reporter was flabbergasted.

Later that night on the evening news, Hill showed the film of Tiger playing golf and commented, "This young man is going to be to golf what Jimmy Connors and Chris Evert are to tennis." Connors and Evert were two teenage tennis stars who were making tennis more popular than it had ever been before.

Now the secret was out. Tiger Woods was a prodigy, a person who demonstrates an amazing talent at an extremely young age.

After the story appeared on the news, Tiger was asked to appear on a nationally broadcast daytime talk show, *The Mike Douglas Show*.

A miniature driving range and green were constructed on the set of the show. The host, Mike Douglas, asked Tiger to shoot and then putt.

After driving the ball expertly into a net, Tiger tried to putt. Three times in a row Tiger putted the ball toward the hole only to watch it roll to the side.

Finally, Tiger turned to the host and complained that the green wasn't very level, and contained a break that was difficult to read.

Douglas was astonished. Although Tiger had missed the shot, he talked about golf like a pro.

Soon after the television appearance, Earl Woods entered Tiger in a nine-hole tournament held at the navy course for boys age ten and under. Most of the boys were at least eight years old. Tiger had just turned two.

He won.

The more Tiger played, the more he enjoyed playing. Earl Woods never, ever had to ask Tiger if he wanted to play or pester him to practice. Instead, Tiger was the one to do the pestering. Almost every day he asked Earl if they were going to go golfing.

By the time he was four years old, Tiger needed a place he could play every day. At the navy course, he had to be accompanied by his father, and Earl Woods had to work. Besides, some club members had started to complain about having Tiger Woods on the golf course. They were embarrassed by the sight of a young African-American child who played golf better than they did. They pressed the club to enforce a rule that stated that no children under the age of ten were allowed to play unaccompanied.

So Kultida Woods decided to help. One day she took Tiger to a nearby course called Heartwell. The course is short and all eighteen holes are par 3s. Still, the golfers who played there were serious about the game. She asked the club's assistant pro, Rudy Duran, if her son could play.

A club pro is an accomplished golfer who helps manage the course and gives lessons to the players who use it. Duran usually spent his time working with middle-aged men.

He told Tida that he would have to watch the boy hit a few balls on the driving range first. If Tiger couldn't play, he didn't want to allow him on the course.

Tiger teed up and with his perfect swing hit a perfect little tee shot. Then he did it again. And again. And again.

After seven shots a wide-eyed Duran motioned for Tiger to stop and told Kultida her son could play whenever he wanted. As he told a reporter later, "I was flabbergasted. He had talent oozing out of his fingertips." Duran later compared Woods to Wolfgang Amadeus Mozart, who was an accomplished composer of classical music at age five. That's how good Tiger was at golf.

Duran became Tiger's first teacher. Working with Earl, they established a special score known as "Tiger par" on each hole so Tiger wouldn't get discouraged if he failed to make regular par. Tiger par on the par-54 course was a 67.

At first, Tiger played the course with only three clubs. But within a year, at age five, Earl gave him a complete set of clubs, all cut down to his size.

He wasn't being pushy. Tiger's game had progressed so far that he really needed all the clubs. While he still didn't hit the ball more than seventy-five or a hundred yards, he knew what he wanted each shot to do. Depending upon the terrain, the condition of the course, and his position, Tiger selected his club accordingly.

He had already developed a feel for the game, something that takes most golfers many, many years. Tiger wasn't just hitting the ball as far as he could and then trying to adjust after that. He was already practicing what is referred to as "course management," planning his approach to each hole and strategically looking two or three shots ahead, in the same way a good chess player does.

Duran and Earl Woods slowly exposed Tiger to more challenging courses. But Tiger didn't get frustrated. No matter how difficult it looked, he studied each hole, thought about each shot in advance, then executed his plan.

Even on eighteen-hole, regulation courses, Tiger was already scoring in the 90s, making him competitive with most of the adult golfers he met. On several occasions, Earl even had to warn Tiger not to make bets with other golfers. He was coming home with his pockets full of one-dollar bills he won on the golf course!

Tiger was becoming something of a local celebrity. He was featured on a popular network television show called *That's Incredible!* where he once again demonstrated his amazing ability. Yet his parents were careful not to allow Tiger to feel that he was better than other kids his age. While they knew he was special, they didn't want him to get a big head.

In fact, sometimes they reminded him that there were some things he wasn't so good at, like baseball. Off the golf course, they made certain to treat him just like any other young boy. Kultida and Earl still read him stories and took him to playgrounds. He liked wrestling with his father, sitting on his mother's lap, and playing with his friends in the neighborhood. As much as possible, they wanted Tiger to have a normal life.

But on his first day of first grade, Tiger became aware that he was different. Not because of the way he played golf, but because of the color of his skin.

On the playground, some older boys grabbed him and tied him to a tree. They threw rocks at him while calling him racial names.

Tiger wasn't hurt and the boys were later caught and punished, but for the first time in his life, Tiger realized that the color of his skin made some people behave differently toward him. He was only five years old, and had already learned much about the game of golf. Now he was growing older, and beginning to learn about real life.

Chapter Three:
1981–1983

The Junior

When Tiger entered school, the role golf played in his life changed. For the past few years he had always been able to play nearly all day long almost every day. But Tiger's parents believed that doing well in school was even more important than playing golf. From the time he first began attending school, they enforced a rule that Tiger couldn't play golf during the week unless all his homework was completed. On weekends, he was allowed to play as much as he wanted, but he still had to complete his schoolwork by Sunday evening.

Tiger was a bright student and did as his parents asked. He had so much fun playing golf that he would do almost anything to get a chance to play.

At about the same time, Earl Woods decided Tiger was ready to play regularly in organized tournaments with other children. He didn't want his son to play with adults all the time, and Tiger's performance in the ten-and-under tournament at the navy course indicated that he was ready for a challenge. Earl Woods knew that the best way to keep Tiger interested in golf was to offer him the opportunity to gauge his progress against others.

Besides, Tiger was always asking Earl for advice on how to improve his game. When the two were on a golf course, Tiger watched other golfers carefully, then discussed their strengths and weaknesses with his father. Tiger pored over instructional books on golf, soaking up information, learning as much from the pictures as he did from the words, which in some cases were beyond his reading level. Tiger even listened to motivational tapes designed to improve his focus and concentration. He was ready to take his game to the next level.

But there is no "Little League" for six-year-old golfers. Instead, there are tournaments for golfers under a certain age. The first level is for golfers age ten and under. Tiger began competing in a series of such tournaments sponsored by the Southern California Junior Golf Association.

Tiger was competitive at these tournaments from the very beginning. On the local level, he began winning immediately. Even though he was usually three or four years younger than the other players and was unable to hit the ball quite as far as they did, Tiger shot far more accurately and was much better around the greens. All of his experience playing to "Tiger par" at Heartwell paid off.

His first major ten-and-under tournament was the Optimist Junior World, played at the prestigious Presidio Hills course in San Diego, California. It was an international tournament, so many of the best young golfers in the world attended.

Tiger was excited about the tournament and the opportunity to travel to San Diego. But he was most excited about the chance to play in the golf tournament.

He was old enough and talented enough that he now had to play by the same rules as everyone else. He no longer teed up every shot. If he mishit a ball and it landed in the rough or was buried in a sand trap, Tiger would have to use all his skill to hit the ball out like everyone else.

He was ready. Years later, Earl Woods enjoyed telling the story about what happened when Tiger was preparing to tee off on the first hole of the tournament.

As Tiger prepared to set the ball on the tee, his father took him aside and told him, "I want you to know I love you no matter what. Enjoy yourself." He didn't want Tiger to think that his father's feelings toward him depended upon how well he played golf.

Then Tiger ripped a tee shot straight down the middle of the fairway. At the end of the round, his father asked him what he had been thinking of as he prepared to tee off at the first hole.

Tiger looked his father in the eye and said, "Where I wanted the ball to go, Daddy." Most golfers, even those who were grown up and experienced, would have answered that question much differently. Many would have responded by saying what they *didn't* want the ball to do. But Tiger was thinking positively.

Although Tiger finished eighth in the field of 150 golfers, he played well. His only problem was that he was still so small that many of the older, stronger boys could simply hit the ball farther than he could. Even though seven boys finished ahead of him, Tiger was the talk of the tournament.

While others coached his son's swing, Earl Woods took responsibility for Tiger's mental approach to the game. His experiences as a Green Beret had taught him how to maintain focus in tense situations.

When he and Tiger played together, Earl Woods tried to distract his son on purpose. For example, just as Tiger would start to putt, his father would cough loudly or step in front of the hole, trying to rattle him. While the tactics bothered Tiger at first, his father explained why he was doing what he did. He wanted to teach his son to concentrate. It wasn't long before Tiger learned to ignore his father's antics. He stayed focused on what he was trying to accomplish.

Earl Woods was beginning to perceive just how special his son was, and how special he could be. He wanted to make certain he was prepared for what the future might hold for him. He realized that Tiger was probably the first African-American, and maybe even the first player of any race, who had ever been exposed to golf at such an early age. For many young boys who play football or baseball while growing up, the basic moves of those sports become automatic. Because Tiger started playing golf while still a toddler, golf's most basic move — the swing — was automatic to him. Tiger played by instinct.

The young boy's situation was made even more unique by Tiger's background. Very few African-Americans played golf, primarily because it was usually played by wealthy people who belonged to private golf clubs. Although there have always been wealthy African-Americans, they were rarely invited to join these private clubs. The few African-Americans who did play, like Earl Woods, often got a late start.

From the very beginning, Earl Woods realized that Tiger's racial background, combined with his talent, made others take notice of him. Although few yet realized it, Tiger wasn't 100 percent African-American. His father was primarily African-American, but his ancestors also included Cherokee Indian. Tiger's mother also came from a racially mixed background. She was half Thai, one-quarter white, and one-quarter Chinese. Although Tiger looked African-American, in reality there was a little bit of everybody in his background. As a result, virtually anyone could identify with him. As his appearances on television had demonstrated, he made people interested in golf who otherwise might not pay much attention to the sport.

Yet there were still some people who felt that African-Americans in general, and Tiger in particular, didn't belong on a golf course. Some private clubs didn't allow African-Americans to join. Others allowed only a few, and they had to be very wealthy.

Although Earl Woods earned a good living, he wasn't rich. He and Tiger usually played on public courses that allowed anyone to play for a small fee. These courses usually weren't quite as attractive to look at or as well kept as many private clubs, but playing on them taught Tiger to adapt to a wide variety of conditions.

As good as Tiger was becoming, at some junior tournaments he was reminded that he was an African-American playing a game dominated by white golfers. On the course, he was under constant scrutiny. His smallest infraction of the rules was certain to be reported. Off the course, other golfers sometimes snubbed him.

Earl and Kultida Woods made certain that their son knew how to react when he experienced racism at the golf course. They taught their son a valuable lesson: "Let your clubs speak for you," they told him. Tiger's parents knew that if Tiger allowed the small-mindedness of others to make him angry or upset, his game would suffer. If that happened, those who thought he didn't belong on the course might seem to be right.

But if Tiger remained calm and let his performance do the talking, he would demonstrate that any human being has a right to be on a golf course. In fact, he might even convince people that everyone has the same rights to all things, not just to golf. Golf was just a game, but in Tiger's hands, it might just prove to be a means to knock down racial barriers.

Chapter Four:
1983–1989

The Champion

Over the next several years the legend of Tiger Woods, golf prodigy, continued to grow. He continued to dominate the Southern California junior golf circuit. Then, in 1983, at age eight, he won his first international event.

It was his third appearance in the Optimist Junior World Tournament. Although he trailed going into the final round, he shot a 5-under-par final round to surge to the top and win. He repeated as champion the following year. With each victory, more people both inside and outside golf became familiar with the name Tiger Woods.

Although he was still in grade school, he occasionally received invitations to participate in clinics and exhibitions given by famous golfers. They enjoyed talking about different golf techniques and then showing everyone that even a young boy could do what they had just described. In one famous instance, Tiger played an exhibition with golfing legend Sam Snead. From the late 1930s through the 1950s, Snead dominated the professional golf tour, winning a then-record eighty-one tournaments. In a lifetime of golf, Snead thought he had seen it all.

Then came Tiger Woods. Snead was amazed as he watched Tiger attempt and make shots that most professional golfers wouldn't even try. But it was Tiger's swing that most impressed the golfing legend.

"I've worked for years to get the hitch out of my swing," commented Snead to a reporter after playing with Tiger, "and along comes this kid. I think I'll toss my clubs in a lake someplace," he joked.

Although Tiger still struggled to hit the ball much over 150 yards, he was so accurate and shot so well around the greens that he played most adult golfers even. On several occasions he was matched against club pros and gave them a scare. More than once, he took the lead on the first nine holes, only to lose on the back nine when the pros finally figured out they were in a real contest and had to bear down.

As Tiger grew older, he became more and more aware of what he might be able to accomplish in golf. One day, he read a magazine article about golfing great Jack Nicklaus, whom many consider the greatest golfer ever. Accompanying the article was a chart that listed how old Nicklaus was when he accomplished certain goals on the golf course. Like Tiger, Nicklaus had been a golf prodigy.

Tiger put the list on his wall and compared himself to Nicklaus. Nicklaus first shot under 50 on a nine-hole course when he was nine years old. Tiger had done so when he was three. Nicklaus broke 80 for an eighteen-hole round at age twelve. Tiger had done so at age eight.

Tiger used the list to create goals for himself. Nicklaus won the Ohio state high school championship at seventeen, the U.S. Amateur at nineteen, and his first major PGA tour event at twenty-two. Tiger looked at the list every day. He dreamed not of just doing as well as Nicklaus had, but of doing better. In his fantasies, he never pretended to be Nicklaus or any other great golfer. Instead, he fantasized about playing against them, and winning.

Competing on the junior golf circuit involved more than just showing up on the golf course. He still practiced almost every day and now took lessons twice a month from an accomplished golf teacher named John Anselmo.

But all the practice in the world would amount to nothing if he couldn't get to the tournament itself. Most of the other junior golfers came from wealthy backgrounds. Their parents could easily afford the course fees for their children's extra practice sessions as well as lessons, and it was no hardship for them to fly around the country to play in national tournaments staged by the American Junior Golf Association.

But Tiger's parents weren't wealthy at all. While they had enough money to live comfortably, the added expense of providing for Tiger's golf career was difficult for them to meet.

Earl Woods did everything he could to help Tiger. In order to pay for everything, he took a second mortgage on the family's house and took out loans. In 1988, when Tiger was twelve, he retired from McDonnell Douglas so he could accompany Tiger to tournaments. He just didn't feel right sending Tiger off by himself at such a young age.

But when people asked Earl if he was doing all that to turn Tiger into a professional golfer, he just scoffed. "It's not necessary for Tiger to become a pro," he once told a reporter. "My goal is for Tiger to be an upright, contributing citizen."

Still, Tiger was forced to fight an uphill battle on the amateur circuit. At most tournaments, Tiger usually arrived the morning the tournament started and went directly from the airport to the golf course. Most other golfers could afford to arrive a day or two earlier, stay at a hotel, and learn the course by playing a few practice rounds.

The resourceful Tiger was able to turn this disadvantage to his favor. On the first round of the tournament, playing the course for the first time, he often fell behind. But he used the first round to learn about the course and the competition. In subsequent rounds he usually improved and was often able to charge from behind. The competition soon learned to play while keeping one eye on the leader board, a scoreboard kept at each hole that showed the top five or six golfers and their scores. As soon as the name Woods appeared, the other golfers knew they were in trouble. They often wilted under pressure as Tiger surged to the lead.

Tiger's reputation grew off the golf course as well. People who knew nothing about golf were intrigued by the African-American prodigy. By the time he entered junior high school, he had been featured on numerous national television programs, like the *Today* show and the evening network news. But he didn't let the appearances go to his head. He remained focused on his goals.

The world of professional golf got its first good look at Tiger when he was fourteen years old. In 1989, he traveled to Arkansas to play in the Insurance Youth Golf Classic, a big event sponsored by the American Junior Golf Association.

As an added incentive to play well, on the last round the junior golfers got to play with a professional. Twenty PGA veterans were recruited to play with the sixty juniors.

On the final round, Tiger played in a group of four golfers, known in golf as a foursome, that included two other junior golfers and professional John Daly. Daly, who was just beginning to make his mark in professional golf and would eventually win the prestigious U.S. Open, was known as one of the longest hitters in golf. His tee shots sometimes traveled nearly 400 yards. In the mind of many observers, Daly was the PGA's next big star.

None of that mattered to Tiger. He was on a golf course, and to him, that meant just one thing: winning.

The two golfers made an interesting pair. Daly was a big man, well over six feet tall and weighing nearly 250 pounds. In contrast, Tiger stood just shy of five and a half feet tall and weighed barely 100 pounds. It looked like a mismatch to have the two players on the same course.

Yet Tiger wasn't intimidated. He jumped out in front of Daly at the beginning of the round. Although Daly hit the ball much farther than he did, Tiger played with far more control, and his touch around the greens put Daly to shame.

After nine holes, Tiger was 3 under par, two shots ahead of Daly. The professional, who spent the front nine laughing and joking with the crowds, stopped smiling. He did not want to be beaten by a child.

Daly closed with a rush, scoring 1 under par, by birdieing three of the last four holes. Tiger, tired after playing golf all weekend, faded and lost to Daly by a stroke.

Still, his performance was the talk of the tournament. Tiger's score was better than those turned in by eight of the twenty pros.

A year later, he proved his performance was no fluke. This time the tournament was played in Fort Worth, Texas, and included twenty-one pros. Tiger's final score of 69 beat eighteen of the professionals, including his playing partner, twenty-seven-year-old pro Tommy Moore.

"I wish I could have played like that at age fourteen," quipped Moore. "Heck, I wish I could play like that at twenty-seven."

At age fourteen, Tiger already played with a 1 handicap. A handicap is a score given to golfers so that those of varying abilities can compete fairly against each other. The lower the handicap, the better the player is presumed to be. A player is given a certain number of strokes, or a handicap, on each round to help him to make par. The handicap number is subtracted from the total number of actual strokes the player took; for example, a player with a 10 handicap who shoots an 82 and a player with a 15 handicap who shoots an 87 actually play to a tie, with a score of 72 for each.

Pro golfers don't get any handicap at all, and a handicap of 10 or less is considered very, very good. Tiger's 1 handicap meant that he was already considered almost equal in skill to a professional.

Even though Tiger was only in junior high, he began hearing from golf coaches at colleges all over the country, all of them eager to have Tiger attend their schools. They knew that if Tiger was on their team, they would have an excellent chance of winning the collegiate championship.

Tiger thought it was funny that he was hearing from colleges before he had even completed eighth grade. But it reminded him of the opportunities golf might provide. Although he dreamed of becoming a professional golfer, he also wanted to go to college. He knew that winning a college scholarship would not only be a way of contributing to his future, it would be a great help to his parents financially. After all, they had already spent most of their savings on his golf career.

Earl Woods continued to do all he could to further his son's amazing talent. To help with Tiger's mental concentration, he employed an old friend from the army, psychologist Jay Brunza, to work with Tiger.

Brunza soon discovered that Tiger concentrated far better than most people. He taught Tiger self-hypnosis so he could get even better.

Not that Tiger seemed to need much help. He was dominating the world of junior golf. By age fourteen he had won more than one hundred tournaments, including five international events, even though he was often the youngest golfer in the field.

As sometimes happens when a young athlete rises to sudden stardom, others began to get jealous of Tiger's success.

Behind his back, people started to whisper bad things about Tiger's father and mother. They had heard stories that several young stars in tennis, gymnastics, and ice skating had suffered breakdowns after being pushed too hard by coaches and parents at too young an age. Many people thought Earl and Kultida Woods were doing the same thing to Tiger. They accused them of not allowing their son to live a normal life.

When Tiger heard such accusations, he laughed. His parents always made it clear to him that if he ever wanted to stop playing golf, that was fine with them. They just wanted him to be happy and to become a good person. So far, playing golf was what Tiger wanted to do. The whole time he was growing up, neither his father nor his mother ever, ever told Tiger that he had to practice. Tiger practiced because he enjoyed it.

Around the house, they treated him just as most parents who love their children treat them, with equal portions of love and discipline. They worked extra-hard to make sure Tiger kept up with his schoolwork. Passing wasn't good enough for Earl and Kultida Woods. Their son had to get all A's.

And once he got off the golf course, Tiger didn't act like a prodigy. Most of his friends didn't play golf. They liked hanging out together, wolfing down fast food, and watching television. In general, he was a well-behaved, well-adjusted boy that any parent would be proud of.

About the most destructive thing Tiger ever did was play golf in the house. He carried a wedge and ball with him almost all the time and teased his mother by lofting soft shots from room to room, narrowly missing vases and glassware. Perhaps that's one of the reasons why he stays so calm out on the golf course today. The pressures of tournament play are nothing compared with having your mother threatening to take away your golf clubs if you break anything!

Tiger's mother has had just as much influence over his development as his father. For if Tiger inherited his drive and determination from Earl Woods, he has inherited his inner strength and sense of calm from his mother.

Kultida Woods was raised as a Buddhist in her native Thailand, and she has always made certain that her son is as aware of his Thai heritage as he is of his African-American roots. When Tiger was nine, she took him to Thailand so he could experience Thai culture for himself, and she has always kept a

Buddhist shrine in the house. Tiger often accompanies his mother on her visits to the Buddhist temple. In fact, when people ask Tiger what his religion is, he responds by saying he is a Buddhist.

Tiger Woods was still just a kid, but he was a teenager whose skill was thrusting him into the adult world and the public eye more and more. Over the next several years, he would grow up fast.

Chapter Five:
1989–1995

The Amateur

At age fourteen, most kids are thinking about their first date. But Tiger Woods was thinking about the fact that the site of the 1990 PGA championship was Shoal Creek Country Club, in Birmingham, Alabama.

Shoal Creek had no African-American members. Although that wasn't a unique situation for a private club, the fact that the PGA had selected that club for its prestigious tournament caused an uproar throughout the nonwhite golfing community. For the first time, the PGA was attacked for being insensitive, and several lucrative commercial sponsors threatened to withdraw their support from the tournament. Eventually, the PGA forced Shoal Creek into accepting black members and announced they would no longer hold any tournaments at courses where blacks were not invited to play.

The media wanted to know what Tiger Woods thought of the controversy.

Tiger tried to avoid the dispute. He was a little uncomfortable when people focused on his African-American heritage and ignored that fact that he was, in fact, more Asian than African-American. Earl Woods tried to explain to his son that in the United States, virtually anyone with any African-American blood is usually perceived as being African-American. He told his son that while there was no need to deny his Asian heritage, in America, people would always view him as an African-American.

But Tiger Woods had never wanted to be the best African-American golfer in history. He wanted to be the best golfer, period.

By the time Tiger entered high school in 1991, it was becoming more and more obvious that he was, in fact, golf's next big star. He was beginning to grow in stature, and his body was catching up to his game.

He dominated the national junior circuit that year. He won the age-fifteen-to-seventeen division of the Optimist Junior World and several other major tournaments, then he capped off the year by becoming the youngest winner of the U.S. Junior Amateur title.

This last victory qualified him for the U.S. Amateur, an event open to golfers of all ages. It was the first time he had competed in the tournament. In the U.S. Amateur, the golfers play through two days of competition. Those with the best scores move on to match play, where they are paired up to compete head-to-head to win individual holes.

Tiger shot a 78 and a 74 the first two days and didn't qualify for match play.

He was disappointed, but not shattered by the loss. After all, he was only fifteen and had a lifetime of golf ahead of him. In the meantime, he was busy playing on his team at Western Hills High School — and off the green, he was busy being a teenager.

He traded in his thick glasses for contact lenses. He started going to parties, dating, and doing everything most kids his age did. At school, Tiger was no big deal. Because he was such a good student, and a little shy, some of them thought he was a bit of a nerd. Most kids knew he golfed, but few realized how good he was. That would soon change.

In 1992, Tiger captured his second U.S. Junior title and again qualified for the U.S. Amateur, played that year at Jack Nicklaus's Muirfield course in Ohio. This year, he hoped to make it to match play.

Tiger shot a 78 on the first round. It seemed he was going to drop out of contention again. Terribly disappointed, that night he went out to a fast-food restaurant and ate ten tacos, his favorite food.

The home remedy must have helped. The next day, he tore up the tough course for a 66, and qualified for match play. Although he didn't make it past the second round, he was getting better.

Tiger began to receive invitations to play as an amateur in professional events. Golf fans wanted to see the emerging star. He accepted and played in a handful of tournaments.

It's an interesting sports phenomenon that athletes often play better and more enthusiastically when they compete against people whose skills are superior to theirs. The challenge is more exciting and the victory sweeter if you don't know you can win easily. Plus, you stand a better chance of improving your game by watching and learning from your opponent. Tiger found this to be true. The more he played with the best golfers in the world, the more his interest in junior golf waned.

Though he found it difficult to get motivated, he still won his third straight U.S. Junior title to qualify for the U.S. Amateur once more. He again lost in the second round of match play.

Tiger soon stopped playing in junior tournaments altogether and began to look ahead. As he progressed through high school, he had to decide where to go to college.

He was recruited by dozens of schools, and finally selected Stanford University. It was a great school, had a fine golf program, and was close enough to home that he would still be able to see his friends, particularly his girlfriend from high school, Deena.

He graduated from high school in June of 1994 and spent the summer competing in national amateur events. He wasn't just playing kids anymore. The big amateur tournaments attracted the best club players in the country. Most of the players were fifteen or twenty years older than Tiger.

It didn't matter. He won anyway. Just before he began his freshman year at Stanford, in late August of 1994, Woods traveled to Florida to compete a fourth time in the U.S. Amateur at the Sawgrass Country Club in Pontre Verde.

This time, Woods planned to win. He was ready. He easily qualified for match play then mowed down the competition to reach the finals. His opponent for the thirty-six-hole match play final was Oklahoma State senior Trip Kuehne, a friend of Tiger's from his junior golf days.

In match play, golfers play for each hole. If a golfer wins a hole, it is referred to as being "one-up." Tie holes don't count. Whoever wins the most holes wins the match.

In the first round, Tiger stumbled early and Trip jumped out to a big lead. He went six-up before Woods recovered to pull to within four at the lunch break after the first eighteen holes.

Then Tiger put on one of his patented finishes. By the 35th hole, he had pulled even.

The par-3 17th hole at Sawgrass is one of the most famous in golf. The green sits on a small island in the middle of a lake, connected to the remainder of the course by only a narrow path. Even the best

Amateur golfer Tiger Woods tees off during a practice round at Augusta, Georgia, in 1995 as professional golfers Ray Floyd (left) and Greg Norman look on.

Earl Woods's happiness for his son's victory at the 1995 Centennial
U.S. Amateur Golf Championship is obvious.

Tiger Woods gives a whoop of celebration when he sends the 1996 U.S. Amateur Championship match into sudden death by tying Steve Scott on the thirty-fifth hole.

With a swing fellow golfers have called "perfect," Tiger tees off at the first hole of the final round of the 1997 Masters.

LEADERS

HOLE	1	2	3	4	5	6	7	8	9	10	11	12	13	14	15	16	17	18
PAR	4	5	4	3	4	3	4	5	4	4	4	3	5	4	5	3	4	4
WOODS	15	16	16	16	15	15	14	15	15	15	16	16	17	18				
ROCCA	6	7	7	7	7	6	6	6	6	6	5	5	5	5				
STANKOWSKI	5	4	3	2	2	2	3	3	2	3	2	2	2	3	3			
KITE T.	4	5	5	4	4	3	4	5	5	5	5	5	6	6	5			
WATSON. T.	5	6	6	6	7	6	3	4	4	5	5	6	6	6	6	5		
SLUMAN	3	3	3	3	2	2	3	3	3	3	3	3	4	5	3	3		
LOVE	0	1	0	0	1	0	0	0	0	0	0	1	3	3	4	3	3	
LANGER	2	1	2	2	2	2	1	0	1	0	0	0	1	1	2	2	2	2
COUPLES	2	3	3	3	2	1	2	2	2	2	2	2	3	1	1	2	3	
TOLLES	0	1	2	2	2	2	2	1	2	2	2	2	3	3	4	5	5	5

The leader board and the throng of spectators tell the story: Tiger Woods is the man to watch at Augusta.

The newly crowned Master receives the famous green jacket from the previous year's winner, Nick Faldo.

An historic building provides a dramatic backdrop to Tiger Woods's tee-off on the Old Course at St. Andrews, Scotland, site of the British Open.

Masters of the game Tiger Woods and Jack Nicklaus strike the same pose while waiting to tee off during the PGA Championship.

Yes! Tiger Woods birdies on the eighteenth hole to force a playoff against Bob May during the final round of the PGA Championship.

Tiger Woods hoists the PGA Championship trophy after winning the three-hole playoff against Bob May.

Tiger Woods's PGA Tournament Wins:

1996:

Las Vegas Invitational

Walt Disney Classic

1997:

Western Open

Byron Nelson Classic

Mercedes Championships

The Masters°

1998:

Bell South Classic

1999:

World Golf Championship—American Express
  Championships

Tour Championship

National Car Rental Golf Classic

World Series of Golf

PGA Championship

Western Open

Memorial Tournament

2000:

Mercedes Championships

AT&T Pebble Beach National Pro-Am

(continued on next page)

Bay Hill Invitational

Memorial Tournament

U.S. Open

British Open

PGA Championship

WGN-NEC Invitational

Bell Canadian Open

*the youngest player ever to win

Tiger Woods's Statistics

Year	PGA Tournaments Entered	PGA Tour Prize Money Won	PGA Rank	Other Tournaments Entered	Prize Money Won	Total Year's Earnings
1996	8	$790,594	24	3	$149,826	$940,420
1997	21	$2,066,833	1	4	$373,998	$2,440,831
1998	20	$1,841,117	4	6	$1,085,889	$2,927,006
1999	21	$6,616,585	1	4	$1,065,040	$7,681,625
2000	17	$8,286,821	1	2	$255,411	$8,542,232
Total	87	$19,601,950		19	$2,930,164	$22,532,114

golfers sometimes plunk several shots in the lake before finding the green.

With the pin placed at the far back corner on the right, common sense said for Woods to play it safe and shoot left, where there was less danger of landing in the water. An errant shot could cost him the match. But Woods played to win.

He hit a wedge and the ball stopped fourteen feet from the hole, only eighteen inches from the water on the back edge of the green. He drilled the putt, then sat back to watch Kuehne. He didn't have long to wait. Kuehne missed his putt for par and conceded the match. At age eighteen, Woods had won the U.S. Amateur.

Now college beckoned. He enjoyed life at Stanford from the beginning. He worked hard, played hard, and played golf hard. His teammates on the Stanford team, Native American Notah Begay, Japanese-American William Yanigasawa, and Chinese-American Jerry Chang, became his best friends. While it was obvious that Woods was the best golfer of the bunch, that didn't stop his teammates from teasing the young freshman.

Once they caught sight of Tiger in his glasses, they razzed him unmercifully, calling him "Urkel" after the bespectacled Steve Urkel character on the TV show *Family Matters*. They also thought he danced awkwardly and often talked him into dancing at parties just so they could make fun of him.

Woods took their good-natured ribbing in stride. He loved the fact that he was just another guy on the team, and virtually anonymous at the school. When he wasn't busy studying for his degree in accounting, he was allowed to have fun like everyone else.

But it was the professional golf career that he had always dreamed of that occupied the bulk of his free time. Now, reaching that dream seemed inevitable.

The win in the U.S. Amateur earned him an invitation to the Masters Tournament at Augusta. Because the event was televised nationally, the average golf fan had an opportunity to get a good look at golf's next big star for the first time. And because Woods was African-American, his appearance was big news.

Tiger made a good first impression. He loved the course and played several stellar practice rounds alongside such stars as Greg Norman, Gary Player, and Nick Price before the tournament began. Inevitably, the tour veterans were struck by his talent.

Tiger now stood more than six feet tall and his weight topped 150 pounds. His short game and putting skills were now supplemented by tee shots that not only were on target, but sometimes traveled well over three hundred yards, equal to those of the best drivers on the pro tour.

In the first two rounds, Tiger made par and made the cut for the first time in a pro event. Though he shot another par on the fourth round, he had ballooned to a 77 on round three, to finish the tournament in forty-first place.

The course had exposed a weakness in his game. His iron play, needed for the second shot on most holes, was erratic. After the tournament, Woods practiced with his irons for hours, working to improve. But many people didn't think it was necessary. They were already saying he should quit school and become a pro.

But Woods still had goals in amateur golf. He remembered what Jack Nicklaus had done before him. He wanted to win the NCAA championship and the U.S. Amateur in the same year, something that only Nicklaus and one other player had ever accomplished.

But as a freshman, he fell short in the NCAA championships, finishing fifth, three shots behind the winner. Yet he stayed focused and in 1995 set his sights on winning a second consecutive U.S. Amateur.

The tournament was played in Newport, Rhode Island, at the demanding Wanumetonomy Golf and Country Club. A second-round 75 was just good enough to qualify him for match play.

On the windy seaside course, he played the breezes like an experienced sailor. Four of his first five opponents conceded before the 18th hole, unable to overcome the insurmountable lead Tiger had built. In the finals, he faced forty-three-year-old tournament veteran Buddy Marucci.

For the first time since match play began, Tiger fell behind. Then, as usual, he mounted a charge. The 17th hole of the final round determined the championship, and Tiger won with a spectacular second shot — a shot that was made with an iron. His hard work was paying off.

With the U.S. Amateur victory behind him, he faced the challenge of his second NCAA championship. Woods was determined to leave Honors Course in Chattanooga, Tennessee, the winner. Not only did he want to duplicate Nicklaus's achievement, he wasn't sure he would be able to play the tournament again.

Although when he started college Tiger fully intended to remain all four years until he graduated, after two years he was now unsure. His growing fame was making it difficult for him. The NCAA had even briefly suspended him for writing an article for a golf magazine, considering it an infraction of their rules. If he did decide to turn pro, he wanted the NCAA individual title before leaving college.

With this motivation, Woods obliterated the competition, one of whom was Nicklaus's son Gary, with opening rounds of 69, 67, and 69 to lead by nine entering the final round. Although he ballooned to an uncharacteristic 80 on the final round, he still won by four strokes and was the only one of 156 competitors to better par for the tournament.

The victory made it virtually certain that he would soon turn pro. Although his parents had hoped he would stay in college all four years and get his degree, even they agreed it was time for him to move on. "I promise you I'll still get my degree," he told them. Yet there was still one last unresolved matter he wanted to take care of — a record-setting third straight victory in the U.S. Amateur.

The tournament began at the Pumpkin Ridge course near Portland, Oregon, in late August of 1996. Tiger opened the tournament with a 69 and a 67 for a total of 136, the best of all sixty-four players in the field.

He proved these scores were no fluke by pounding his competition into the ground as he reached the finals for the third year in a row. His opponent in the thirty-six-hole final would be University of Florida sophomore Steve Scott. For one of the few times in his life, Woods was actually older than his opponent, twenty to Scott's nineteen.

The pugnacious Scott wasn't intimidated by his rival. He had battled Woods in junior competition.

Instead, it was Woods who appeared intimidated. He double-bogeyed the 2nd hole, and after only five holes, Scott had won three to go three-up. He continued his fine play while Woods struggled. At the lunch break, Scott led five-up.

For virtually any other golfer on the planet, and certainly every other amateur, 5-up with only eighteen holes to play would be an insurmountable lead to overtake. But Tiger Woods isn't like other golfers.

Scott kept the pressure on by hitting his second shot on the 19th hole off the flagstick. Meanwhile, Woods landed in the rough. But Scott missed a birdie putt and Woods scrambled for a par. The score remained the same.

Then Woods found his stride. He birdied on holes 21, 22, 23, and 27 to draw to within one as the two young golfers headed for the back nine. As Tiger's play strengthened, Scott's slipped.

But he regrouped and birdied the next hole to go back to two-up. Then Tiger eagled the par-5 29th hole. Scott birdied, but still lost the hole. Yet he pushed his lead back to two-up with a birdie on 32. The lead held through 33.

Then Tiger scored two consecutive birdies, the last on a grand, rolling, thirty-foot putt. The score was tied going into the final hole. Both golfers parred to send the competition into sudden death.

Woods and Scott made easy pars once again on the first hole. The next, a par 3, proved the difference.

Woods got on the green safely with his first shot, while Scott landed in the rough. Scott pitched to a few yards past the hole.

Putting for a birdie, and the match, Tiger slid his twelve-foot putt eighteen inches past the pin.

Now Scott putted. His putt also skidded past the hole.

Woods lined up his shot carefully. He pulled back, and with a gentle touch, tapped in — and won his third straight U.S. Amateur victory!

The final was one of the greatest in amateur golf. Woods's comeback from a five-point deficit was the stuff legends are made of.

A gracious Scott summed up the feelings of perhaps every golfer Woods had ever played against as an amateur when he asked after the tournament, "What does it take to beat this guy?"

There was no answer, at least in the amateur golf circuit. Soon, the professionals would learn if they had what was necessary to defeat Tiger Woods.

Chapter Six:
1996

The Professional

With his record-setting third straight U.S. Amateur title added to his list of accomplishments, Woods made official what everyone had been speculating about for weeks. He became a professional golfer.

Immediately after his win, he was whisked to the corporate tent sponsored by Nike and met with his agent, Hughes Norton. A few hours later he flew on a Nike corporate jet to Milwaukee. He had decided to make his professional debut at the Greater Milwaukee Open, one of seven professional-amateur tournaments remaining in the 1996 PGA season for which Tiger had requested permission to play as an amateur. Given his recent performance and growing stature in the world of golf, the tournaments were delighted to have him.

The public was still unaware of Woods's plans. He had originally entered the tournament as an amateur, and planned to announce his intention to turn pro on Wednesday, after playing in the tournament's pro-am event. But when word began to leak out that he was turning pro, Woods moved the announcement ahead by one day. On the Tuesday before the tournament, he released a brief statement that read simply, "This is to confirm that, as of now, I am a professional golfer."

He chose the Milwaukee tournament as his first professional event with the same care and focus he used on the golf course. The Greater Milwaukee Open, played in Glendale, Wisconsin, at the Brown Deer Park golf course, was not one of the PGA's premier events. Few of the top players were entered. That was fine with Woods. He wanted to make his debut with as little hoopla as possible. Playing in a minor tournament allowed him the leisure to break into the professional ranks without undergoing too much scrutiny.

Tiger had a plan in mind for his first months as a pro. In the seven pro tournaments he planned to play in before the end of 1996, he hoped to earn enough money to become one of the top 125 money winners on the tour. If he did so, he would automatically earn membership in the PGA for the following year. He would not have to play in the tough qualifying rounds preceding each tournament that many fledgling pros are forced to compete in in order to play.

But Tiger quickly learned that it would be impossible for him to be just another golfer on the tour. The general public soon learned that he had signed two endorsements deals, one with Nike and one with Titleist, a golf equipment manufacturer, that were worth a total of more than sixty million dollars! Before playing a single round of professional golf, Woods was already certain to receive enough money to live on for the rest of his life. The deal was worth more than most professional golfers ever dreamed of making in their entire lives.

Some pros were already jealous, and sniped about Woods behind his back. As one fellow pro commented snidely, "I think it's going to be a little easier for him to make that last putt knowing he has sixty million in the bank." Yet most realized that Woods was good for golf's status in the world of sports. They believed that any added attention his presence brought to the game would benefit every-one on the tour.

The Greater Milwaukee Open tournament began on Thursday, September 5. As Tiger approached the first tee, even he was stunned by the sight.

The first hole, a fairway some 450 yards long, was surrounded by a huge throng of people. When they saw Woods, they let up a mighty roar.

The two other pros scheduled to play with Woods, Jeff Hart and John Elliott, were taken aback. Both were relative newcomers to the tour and totally un-prepared for crowds.

As Woods placed the ball on the tee and ad-dressed it, preparing to take his first shot as a pro-fessional, the outside world faded away. Just as at his first big amateur tournament, the Optimist World Junior when he was only six years old, a single thought crossed his mind. He focused on where he wanted the ball to go.

The crowd grew still as Woods took aim on the ball. Then he spun back, lifted the club far behind his head, and exploded into the ball, his follow-through spinning his upper body back around. He then paused, the club hanging over his left shoulder, and looked down the fairway.

As soon as the ball left the ground, some people in the crowd began to clap and cheer. Then, as they saw exactly where and how far the ball was going, the cheers turned into a mighty din.

Far down the fairway, nearly 300 yards away, Woods's ball landed just to right of center and began to roll. It came to rest 336 yards from the tee. Under any conditions, it was an amazing shot. As his first professional drive, it was absolutely astounding.

Woods now stood six-two and weighed about 175 pounds. His shoulders were wide and his legs long. He was built more like an NBA point guard than a professional golfer. He was able to generate tremendous power. He made the other pros look soft and out of shape.

After the first shot, any pressure Woods felt evaporated. The game held his entire concentration. He made a par 4 on the first hole, then made back-to-back birdies on holes 3 and 4. He finished the back nine with a score of 31, 4 under par. He was among the leaders.

After starting the back nine with a string of pars, Woods then closed with a rush, birdieing the last two holes to finish with a score of 67, 4 under par on the par-71 course.

The other pros were impressed. Some observers thought Woods had a good chance of winning the tournament.

He followed with a second round of 69 to go 6 under par for the tournament before reality set in. Although Tiger was playing well, the leader after two rounds was already *14* under par.

Tiger could not keep up the pace. He finally crashed from exhaustion during round three, shooting a 73 to take himself out of contention for the championship. He then recovered with a 68 to finish the tournament at 6 under par, a good score, but far behind winner Loren Poole. Woods finished in sixtieth place, and earned only $2,544.

Yet Woods was ecstatic. His winnings represented the first paycheck he had ever earned by playing golf, and meant more to him than the pending sixty million dollars in endorsement deals. He had enjoyed himself immensely during the week, and was like a kid in a candy store as he showed his father all the free equipment — bags and balls and golf shirts — he had received from the tournament sponsors. Even sitting in the clubhouse after each round and talking to the other pros had been fun. He was finally where he belonged.

"It's great to just get back to what I do: play golf," he told a reporter. "That's what I know best. That's what I've always done."

The following week he played in the Canadian Open. He would be facing better competition than in the Greater Milwaukee Open, and everyone wondered how Woods would adjust.

They needn't have worried. Rain limited the tournament to only three rounds. Woods's final round of 68 was best of the day and good enough to lift him into eleventh place.

His next stop on tour was the Quad City Classic in Coal City, Illinois. Like the Greater Milwaukee Open, it was a minor stop on the tour. The big golf story that week was supposed to be the President's Cup, a premier event that matched some of the best American golfers against an international team.

But the golf world had found their new hero and he was playing in Illinois. They all but ignored the

President's Cup and focused their attention on Woods after he opened the tournament with rounds of 69 and 64 to take a one-stroke lead. His 69 on the third day was good enough to keep him on top.

In his amateur career, Woods had never lost a tournament in which he led going into the final round. If he could keep up the momentum, the tournament was his to win.

But on one of the early holes, he shot his way into trouble. From the tee of the par-4 4th hole, he intended to hit a "fade," a shot that drifts to the right. Properly done, the shot would leave Woods with a perfect approach to the green.

Woods swung, but instead of hitting a fade he rushed through the ball and pulled it. It soared high and long, but hooked wildly to the left.

Kerplunk! The ball landed in a small pond along the fairway.

Woods tried not to get rattled. When a ball lands someplace where it can't be played, golfers are allowed to take a "drop." They receive a one-stroke penalty but are allowed to drop another ball near where the unplayable shot finished and continue their round.

Woods dropped the ball at the edge of the pond. A large tree blocked his way to the green.

Woods looked at the ball and then out toward the green, mulling over his options. He could play it safe and hit the ball back toward the fairway, setting up an easy shot to the green, but he would have to settle for at least a bogey on the hole. Or he could still try to salvage par.

There was a small opening between tree branches. Woods realized he could save par if he punched the ball between the branches and onto the green. It was dangerous, but possible.

Woods made his decision. He wanted to win.

He took dead aim and shot the ball toward the gap between the branches. He missed.

The ball hit a limb squarely and rocketed back over his head.

Kerplunk! He was back in the water.

After taking another drop, Woods played it safe, but the additional penalty stroke and a two putt left him with an eight for the hole, a quadruple bogey!

Although he played well for the remainder of the round, the shot cost him a win. He finished fifth.

A week later he finished third in the B.C. Open in Endicott, New York, earning almost sixty thousand dollars. In only four short weeks, Woods had earned $140,194, making him 128th on the tour money list.

All around the country, golf writers and fans were going overboard praising golf's newest sensation. He wasn't just good, he was great! After only one month of play, he was already being compared to the greatest golfers of all time: Arnold Palmer, Jack Nicklaus, and Greg Norman, among others. Yet as great as these men were, none of them had begun his professional career as auspiciously as Woods.

But Tiger soon discovered that there was more to being a professional golfer than just playing well. Now he had to worry about what he did off the course as well.

Although he was scheduled to play in the Buick Challenge in Pine Mountain, Georgia, the following week, Woods was exhausted. Including the U.S. Amateur, he had been playing golf almost nonstop for six weeks. So after shooting a disappointing practice round the day before the tournament was to begin, he withdrew and returned to his new home in Orlando, Florida.

Although tournament officials were disappointed, Woods's withdrawal wasn't an issue. But he also decided to skip an awards dinner at which he was scheduled to be given the Fred Haskins Award, collegiate golf's highest honor. Because Woods pulled out, the dinner was canceled and several hundred people had to change their plans at the last minute. The tournament sponsor lost $30,000 for a dinner that was never held.

Woods was strongly criticized for skipping the dinner. Some golfers agreed with pro Peter Jacobson, who said, "You can't compare him to Nicklaus and Palmer anymore, because they never did this."

Even Palmer thought Woods had made a mistake, adding, "He should have played and he should have gone to the dinner. You don't make commitments you can't fulfill."

Woods realized his mistake, and quickly made a public apology. He even sent a personal letter to each person who was scheduled to attend the dinner. The controversy was over, but Woods knew he would have to work twice as hard to restore his image. He didn't want people to think he was uncaring — he just hadn't considered the conse-quences of his actions. With the way Tiger Woods tore up a golf course, people sometimes forgot that he was only twenty years old. He was still learning, both on and off the golf course.

Chapter Seven:
1996

The Winner

After resting for a week and trying to mend fences with the media and his fellow tour professionals, Woods traveled to Nevada for the Las Vegas Invitational. The event would prove to be a good gauge of his progress.

His quick start in his first four tournaments was one of the best in PGA history. Everyone was anticipating his first win, even his own family. After Tiger withdrew from the Buick Challenge, Earl Woods told several people that his son was going to win in Las Vegas.

Yet unlike most PGA tournaments, the Las Vegas Invitational is a five-round event played on three different courses. While none is particularly difficult, the odd arrangement makes the tournament a notoriously difficult one to handicap. Virtually every player in the field has a realistic chance to win. Although Woods was looking for his first tour victory, he would have to play ninety near-perfect holes of golf in order to do so.

In the first round, played at the Las Vegas Country Club, Woods dug himself into a hole. In the thin desert air of Las Vegas, Woods's already towering drives often soared thirty or forty yards longer than usual. As a result, he was shooting himself past the best position from which to approach the tee. He scrambled to finish at 70, a decent round, but one that left him far behind the leaders.

The situation was eerily similar to that which he had so often experienced in amateur competition: his slow start would gradually gain momentum until he blew away the competition at the end. Woods had always believed that, like a sprinter in a race against a long distance runner, his opponent might be able to beat him in a single round, but in multiround competitions he was almost impossible to beat. The five-round format at Las Vegas offered just such an opportunity.

On day two he adapted to the Las Vegas climate. He gained control of his tee shots and was able to adjust his second shot to reach the green in good shape. Even the longest par 5s were no match for Woods, as he made many of the greens in only two shots.

He finished the round with a spectacular 63. Had he putted with his accustomed authority, he might well have shot 60 or better, but the lightning-fast greens were slick, and he missed several easy-to-make putts.

The round got everyone's attention. In the clubhouse afterward, golfers described Tiger's play to one another in disbelief. Upon learning that on some holes that measured nearly 600 yards, Woods had reached the green in only two shots, they rolled their eyes and shook their heads in wonder. No one else on the tour could do that.

The round pulled Woods to within seven shots of the lead. After shooting a 68 on day three, he still trailed by six, but a fourth-round 67 pulled him to within four. Only eighteen holes of golf remained.

The final round began with a 408-yard par-4 hole. He got off to a quick start, easily reaching the green in two then rolling in a fifteen-foot putt for a birdie. Then, on the 492-yard par-5 3rd hole, Woods again reached the green in two and aced a long putt for an eagle three. He finished the back nine with a 31 and was closing on the lead.

After making par on the 10th hole, Woods took aim at the 448-yard 11th. But he overshot his tee shot and the ball landed in a bunker on the side of the fairway.

For most golfers, that meant serious trouble. The bunker was too far from the green to use a wedge for the next shot, and playing an iron, the only club with which most golfers could reach the hole from the spot, was asking for trouble. An iron shot, coming in at a low angle, was certain to run right off the slick greens.

Tiger wasn't like most golfers. He hit the ball farther than anyone, and was often able to use a club no one else dreamed of using. Standing above his ball about one hundred yards from the front of the green, Woods looked at his caddie, Mike "Fluff" Cowan, and asked for his wedge.

Golf fans in the gallery were stunned. The sand wedge usually was used when a golfer was buried in a sand trap and had to dig the ball out of the soft surface and loft it twenty or thirty yards onto the green. The distance Tiger was planning to cover was three times that.

But Tiger Woods knew what he was doing. He had practiced shots like this before. He knew he could hit a wedge one hundred yards. Besides, even if the ball didn't make it all the way, there was little chance that he would overshoot the hole. Not even Tiger Woods could hit a sand wedge that far. For Woods, the shot made sense. For any other golfer, it was pure insanity.

Tiger stood over the ball and took a backswing longer and slower than he usually did with a wedge. Then he swung through the ball with all the power he could muster.

Thwock! The club head hit the ball, and dirt and grass flew into the air as he followed through, his eyes looking toward the green. The ball rocketed toward the hole, impossibly high and long for a wedge. It hit the ground and rolled with enough speed to make it over the edge of the rough and settle onto the edge of the green. The ball stopped thirty feet from the pin.

The gallery exploded with cheers, sounding more like the crowd at a basketball game when a player hits a key three-pointer with time running out than like the typically reserved golf spectators.

When Tiger approached the ball, he barely paused before rolling it home. He had turned an almost certain bogey into a backbreaking birdie. The shot brought him to 5-under for the day, and 24-under for the tournament. First place was within reach.

He birdied three of the next four holes and finished with a score of 64, a total of 27 under par. Of all the golfers who had finished playing, Woods led.

But other golfers were still out on the course. Davis Love III, one of the tour's best players, was even with Woods. While Tiger stayed loose on the practice tee, Love missed a birdie putt on the 18th hole to remain tied. The two would play a sudden death playoff for the championship.

Only a few weeks before, during a practice round, Woods had mentioned to Love that he thought it would be fun to go head-to-head against one another for a tournament victory. Now, Tiger had all the fun he could handle.

As the two men approached the tee on the par-4 1st hole of the playoff, everyone in golf wondered how Woods would react to the pressure. As most golfers knew, winning on the amateur circuit was one thing. All the golfers on the PGA tour had been great amateurs. But winning a PGA event, with thousands of dollars at stake, was something else entirely. Many otherwise fine players simply couldn't handle such pressure.

Love shot first, and drove the ball far and long down the fairway. As Woods teed up, most expected him to outdrive Love.

But the playoff was not unlike amateur match play, at which Woods had excelled. When two golfers go head-to-head, the competition is as much mental as it is physical. Tiger Woods had spent a lifetime preparing for such a situation.

He shot a three wood, and the ball soared through the air in a virtual mirror image of Love's shot. But at the last moment it fell short, and stopped just a few yards short of Love's ball.

The shot was no accident. Woods knew that the player farthest from the hole had to shoot first. He was so confident that he purposely stayed shorter than Love so he could shoot the second shot first. The tour rookie wanted to put pressure on the veteran.

Tiger's plan worked to perfection. He hit his second shot pin-high, only eighteen feet from the hole.

Now Love had to shoot knowing that Woods had a very makable putt for a birdie. He pulled his second shot and narrowly missed a water hazard before the ball lodged in a bunker at the back of the green. He would have to scramble to save par.

Because Love was farther from the hole, now he shot first. He blasted a fine shot from the bunker, but the ball rolled six feet past the hole. If Woods could sink his putt for a birdie, he would win.

Woods spent a few moments carefully considering the shot. He looked at the putt from several angles, trying to gauge the undulating surface of the green and judge the speed and break his putt would need to drop in the hole. Then he stood over the ball, and as absolute silence settled in on the green, he tapped the ball with his putter.

The crowd started cheering immediately, the volume escalating as the ball neared the hole. Then, just as it reached a fever pitch, the ball slowed and stopped two feet short. Woods had been too cautious. The gallery groaned.

Yet because he was so short, he was allowed to tap in. He made par.

The pressure was back on Love. If he sank the six-footer, the two golfers would have to play another hole. If he missed, he lost.

Tiger Woods stood to Fluff Cowan's side at the edge of the green, watching Love line up the putt and bend over the ball. On every side, hundreds, perhaps a thousand golf fans pressed in on the edges of the green, deadly silent, aware that they were in a position to witness history.

Love slowly moved the putter back, then smoothly struck the ball. It rolled toward the cup, slowed, then stopped, inches from the hole.

The crowd exploded. Tiger Woods had won!

A bright, wide smile broke loose on Tiger's face as Love reached out his hand in congratulations. Then Tiger looked into the crowd for his mother.

Kultida Woods came sprinting out from the throng and threw her arms around her son's neck.

Tiger Woods had won.

Chapter Eight:
1996

Tiger's World

Tiger's amazing start and first tour win changed the game of golf, if not for all time, at least for the foreseeable future. He instantly became the most popular and most famous golfer in the world.

The years of anticipation that preceded his professional career were suddenly and spectacularly fulfilled. Longtime golf fans and touring pros were equally impressed. Woods wasn't just good; he was great. He did things on the golf course that no other golfer dreamed of. Not only did he hit the ball long, but his touch around the green was unmatched.

Yet none of this explains the public's fascination with Tiger Woods. Like Babe Ruth in the sport of baseball, or Michael Jordan in basketball, Woods appears to be precisely the right player at the right time for the game of golf. His personal charisma has made the game more popular than ever.

The reasons for this are complex. Before Woods, golf was always perceived as a game played primarily by wealthy, middle-aged white men. Most Americans felt they had little in common with the average professional golfer. There were a few occasional exceptions, like the entertaining and talented Mexican-American golfer Lee Trevino, a dominant player in the 1970s, but Trevino was never able to transcend the sport.

Woods has. He wasn't raised on the links of a country club. He learned the game on public courses. And he is young, with a mile-wide smile and an inviting personality. In comparison, most other professional golfers seem bland.

His unique heritage has helped create these perceptions. In the entire history of golf, only a few African-Americans have made a mark on the professional tour. Not until the 1960s did the PGA even allow African-Americans to compete. Back in the 1940s, Teddy Rhodes was one of the best golfers in the world, but because of his skin color he often wasn't allowed to display his talent. When the PGA became integrated in the 1960s and 1970s, African-Americans Charles Sifford, Jim Dent, and Calvin Peete enjoyed some success, but like Tiger's father, Earl, each man had discovered golf late. They were never fully able to harness their talent.

Tiger Woods is everyman. For as he constantly reminds people, he is not only an African-American. He is also Asian, Native American, and Caucasian. Almost everyone can identify with Tiger. In his face one can see the world.

Of course none of this would matter if Woods didn't have the talent to back up his other gifts. But he does. He entered professional golf as the most ballyhooed amateur ever, and his performance thus far lived up to the hype. And at the time of his win at Las Vegas, he was only twenty years old. The thought that Woods might still be improving is an idea that golf fans find thrilling.

Perhaps the biggest problem facing Woods as a professional has nothing to do with his golf game. Almost overnight, he went from being a person who slept in a dorm room, went to fraternity parties on the weekend, dashed into a fast-food restaurant whenever he wanted, and had to ask his parents for pocket change, to one of the wealthiest and most recognizable people in the world of sports.

Many professional athletes of Woods's age with far less money and fame have discovered that they were ill prepared to deal with the consequences of such good fortune. Many have collapsed under the pressure to perform and never fulfilled their promise. Some have just burned out and discovered they no longer enjoyed the sport that brought them so much. Others have succumbed to drugs or alcohol, or allowed an indulgent lifestyle to rob them of their drive and determination to succeed.

From the very beginning, Woods has tried to avoid these pitfalls. It started with his parents.

When Tiger was growing up, Earl and Kultida Woods bent over backward to prepare their son for his future. They didn't push him into golf or treat him as if he were special. They made certain he was well rounded and emphasized his education. Whenever anyone bothered to ask what gave them the most pride in their son, they inevitably responded that they were most proud of the fact that he had turned into a thoughtful, intelligent, and unassuming young man. Golf was secondary.

This strong foundation has allowed Woods to remain himself. While money and fame have brought some inevitable changes to his life, he tries to act and behave like the same old Tiger.

If anything, these changes have made him a better person. He has had to grow and learn to accept responsibility for his actions. He realizes his importance to the game of golf, his status as a role model, and his obligations to others.

Even before he turned pro, Woods went out of his way to try to give something back to the game and to his fans. He appeared in countless clinics and exhibitions, and he continues to do so. After becoming a professional, he even established his own charitable organization, the Tiger Woods Foundation, to help children all over the world.

He has had a great deal of help in making this sudden adjustment to celebrityhood. Basketball player Michael Jordan, who underwent a similar transformation more than a decade ago, has become a close friend. He and Woods have met at length on several occasions, and Woods has asked Jordan for advice on how to deal with crowds and the pressures of being a public person. Ken Griffey Jr. is a neighbor of Woods's in Florida and has likewise become a valued friend and adviser.

But his fellow touring pros have probably provided the most help. While a jealous few may criticize him unfairly, most other PGA members, like his neighbor Mark O'Meara, have been eager to offer counsel, occasional criticism, or even just play a friendly round of golf. Golf legends like Arnold Palmer and Jack Nicklaus have been similarly forthcoming. They look at Woods with admiration and want him to succeed because they love golf and know what his success can do for the future of the game.

Yet Woods still found tour life a bit isolating. Moving from hotel to hotel week after week was rough. Earl Woods, who had always accompanied his son to every tournament when he was an amateur, now stayed away sometimes in order to assist with Tiger's business affairs. In fact, he had missed the win at Las Vegas. He knew his son had to learn to get by on his own.

At age twenty, Woods was by far the youngest player on the tour. The average age of most players was early thirties. Woods could talk golf with these men, but that was about it. They shared few of his other interests, like rap music and video games. There was no one for him to hang out with and have fun.

So one day, he called his old friend from Stanford, teammate Jerry Chang, and asked him to join him. Chang agreed, and now often accompanies Woods on tour.

Woods's auspicious professional start opened up a world of opportunity. His ability was unquestioned, and thus far he appeared able to handle the demands of his life. Only one question remained.

What would Tiger Woods do next?

Chapter Nine:

1997

The Man

After the win at Las Vegas, Tiger Woods regrouped. His victory earned him the much-valued PGA exemption from qualifying for the remainder of 1996 and for the following two years as well. With that accomplished, his next goal came easily. All Woods wanted to do was win.

But with tour earnings of over $400,000 for the year, Woods now had a shot to finish in the tour's top thirty money winners. If he did, he would qualify for the final event of the tour season, the Tour Championship, an event that only the best golfers of the year were allowed to play in.

A week after Las Vegas he competed in the Texas Open. After two rounds below par, he ballooned to a 73 in the third round and fell seven shots back.

Seven shots back is a deficit that would cause many players to crumble. But Woods is never more dangerous than when he is behind. Entering the final round, he decided he needed to shoot a 64 to win the event.

He almost did, drawing to within one shot of the leader after fifteen holes. But on the 16th he missed a short putt for a birdie that would have vaulted him into a tie for the lead, then missed the green with his tee shot on the par-3 17th and bogeyed the hole to fall back. He won $81,600, but finished third.

At a press conference after the tournament, a reporter began a question by praising Woods for his third-place finish.

Woods cut him off. "The idea," he pointed out, "is to win the darn thing." Nothing else mattered to him.

He proved that in his next tournament, the Walt Disney World/Oldsmobile Classic played in Orlando, near his new home. But despite being on his own turf, Woods was anything but comfortable when he began the tournament.

A bout with bronchitis made him feel weak. He thought about withdrawing but, remembering the problems backing out had caused the year before, decided not to. His presence at a tournament sent the number of spectators and the television ratings soaring. Besides, a commitment was a commitment.

He opened with an admirable 69, but several other golfers had scored a 63, which left Woods six shots back. That night, as he later told reporters, he looked at his visiting father and said, "Pop, I'm gonna shoot a sixty-three tomorrow and get back in this thing."

Woods had an early starting time the following day. When he returned home after his round, his father was just getting out of bed.

"What did you shoot, son?" he asked.

"A sixty-three," responded Tiger. He was "back in the thing."

For his last two rounds, Woods was followed by an increasingly large and boisterous gallery. Thus far in his career, his popularity was best gauged by television ratings points and sales of Nike products. His gallery had been large, but not dramatically bigger than those of other golfers.

All that now changed. It seemed as if every fan on the course wanted to follow Woods. At the first tee, he was surrounded by so many people that they lined the fairway all the way to the green. Tournament organizers soon began providing extra security for Woods just to control the crowds.

But it was more than the size of Tiger's gallery that made it unique. It was the composition. Golf crowds usually looked much like the golfers they followed — white, wealthy, middle-aged, and male.

Tiger's gallery certainly had its share of these fans. But there were others besides.

The crowds following Woods were much younger. More African-Americans were in the gallery than anyone could ever remember seeing at a golf tournament before. Young women nearly outnumbered middle-aged men. The throng looked more like that of a rock concert than a golf tournament.

They also sounded and behaved different. Many had never before attended a golf tournament and weren't familiar with course etiquette. Experienced golf fans know to remain silent as a golfer prepares to shoot, and not to approach golfers between shots. Woods's fans were new to the game.

Experienced gallery members had to constantly hush the newcomers before each shot, and as Woods walked down the course, fans surged toward him, trying to slap him on the back or shake his hand. And after each shot, good or bad, they roared and cheered and called out his name as if he had just hit a game-winning home run in baseball's World Series. "You the man!" became the singular catch-phrase used by crowds to cheer on Woods.

Woods didn't really mind the distractions, and observers noted that if the game of golf wanted to expand its base, then some change in the decorum of the gallery was to be expected. But some longtime fans groused at the transformation and gave up trying to follow Woods. They weren't certain they liked all the changes that were taking place.

Woods shot another 69 on the third round to remain in contention. On the final day, he closed with a 66 — and won for the second time in two weeks, finishing 21 under par.

It was no longer possible to compare Woods to other golfers on the tour. He had vaulted past them. The press flipped through the record books to try to put Tiger's accomplishments in perspective.

Of his first seven professional tournaments, Woods had finished in the top ten in five. The great Jack Nicklaus was considered to have had one of the most precocious starts in professional golf. Yet in his first ten tournaments, he had finished in the top ten only once.

It wasn't even fair just to compare Woods to other young golfers anymore. He was already accomplishing things on the golf course that were the stuff of history. In fact, his victory in Orlando concluded one of the best stretches of golf any player had ever had. Of his last twenty-one rounds, eighteen had been below 70. His scoring average was 67.89, the lowest in history and good enough to win the Vardon Trophy, given to the golfer with the lowest average each year, if Woods had played enough tournaments to qualify. He also led the tour in driving average, with more than 302 yards per tee shot, and birdies per round, with nearly five.

Most golfers and golf writers ran out of words to describe him. Tour veteran Peter Jacobson summed up the feelings of many when he said after the tournament, "If this is how it is every week, then it's over. He is the greatest golfer in the history of the game."

Woods himself was unimpressed. In the press conference after the win, he said matter-of-factly, "I haven't really played my best golf yet." He summed up his performance thus far by adding, "There's room for improvement."

Those words sent shudders down the spine of every PGA professional. If that was true, they all would soon be playing for second place.

Yet there were still a few golf fans and fellow professionals who were not quite convinced of Woods's infallibility. His streak had come on a series of relatively easy courses that Woods's long-ball game seemed made for. And many top pros skip most year-end tournaments, so Woods's achievements weren't always made against the best possible competition.

It would be different at Woods's next tournament, the Tour Championship in Tulsa, Oklahoma. The course was tough and demanding, and the field top-notch. In his brief pro career, this was his biggest challenge.

The raucous crowd that had seemed to appear from nowhere at Orlando was back at the Tour Championship. When Woods teed off on the first hole with fellow pro Brad Faxon, the entire hole, from tee to green, was framed in by fans. He scrambled to a bogey, made two birdies later in the round, then finished with another bogey on the 18th hole to score an even-par 70.

But no one was tearing up the tough course. The good, but not great, round left Woods at even par, yet only four strokes off the lead.

That night, Woods and his parents stayed in separate rooms at a hotel near the golf course. At 2 A.M. Friday morning, Earl Woods woke his wife and told her he was having chest pains.

A heavy smoker, Woods's father had undergone heart surgery ten years earlier. Kultida Woods was taking no chances. She called for an ambulance, and her husband was rushed to a hospital. He was having a mild heart attack. Fortunately, doctors didn't think he was in immediate danger.

Only when she was sure Earl was going to be okay did she call for her son. Although she told him to go back to sleep so he would be rested for the third round of the tournament, Woods rushed to the hospital and stayed until dawn. Then, at his parents' insistence, he went back to the golf course for the third round.

A distracted Woods shot a 78 as his thoughts remained with his father. Although his mother left the hospital and told her son his father was going to be fine, Woods couldn't concentrate. As soon as the round ended, he rushed back to the hospital, telling reporters in the clubhouse as he dressed that "I didn't want to be here today because there are more important things in life than golf. I love my dad to death."

When he reached the hospital he found a somewhat perturbed, grouchy patient who was already anxious to leave. Earl Woods had even felt well enough to watch the third round on television. He didn't want to talk about his health. He wanted to talk about his son's game.

Satisfied that his father would recover, Woods concluded the tournament with a 72 and a 68 to finish in twenty-first place. In a sense, Woods's critics had been correct. The Tour Championship had tested him. But although he hadn't won the tournament, most agreed that, given the near-tragedy in his personal life, he passed the test with flying colors.

With the tour season over, Woods cleared up some unfinished business. He returned to Georgia and attended a rescheduled dinner at which he finally received the Haskins Award. In his acceptance speech, he was unabashedly apologetic.

"My actions were wrong," he said. "I'll never make that mistake again."

He finished the year by participating in the Australian Open, where he finished fifth. Then he played in the Skins Game.

The Skins Game is a made-for-television event matching four golfers who play head-to-head against each other for a "skin," or a sum of money worth from twenty to sixty thousand dollars for each hole. If a single golfer wins the hole outright, he wins the skin. If not, the money is added to the value of the next hole. Potentially, a single shot can be worth hundreds of thousands of dollars.

Fred Couples won the event by earning $280,000. Tiger won only $40,000, but the match was one of the highest-rated televised golf events ever, with twice as many viewers tuned in as the previous year. The reason, of course, was Tiger Woods.

In only a few short months he had already accomplished more on the PGA tour than most golfers do in an entire career. And he was just getting started. There was more he wanted to do.

Chapter Ten:
1997

The Master

On December 30, 1996, Tiger Woods turned twenty-one years old. He ended the year as the most talked-about personality in sports, certainly the first time a golfer ever held that distinction. A few weeks later, Woods began play on the 1997 PGA tour.

Now that he was expected to win, many of his fellow golfers and members of the press wondered if he would be able to rise to the challenge. Woods provided them with an immediate answer.

In his first event, the Mercedes Championship played in Carlsbad, California, in mid-January, Woods checked in with a classic performance.

As usual, he started slowly, then built momentum. He began round three trailing leader Tom Lehman by four strokes.

The veteran Lehman was no pushover. In fact, he was coming off his best year as a pro, and one of the best years by anyone on the tour in years. In 1996 he had earned a tour-leading $1,780,159, won the British Open and several other tournaments, captured the Byron Nelson Award as scoring leader with an average round of 69.32, and was selected as the 1996 Player of the Year. So far, Lehman was playing like he planned to win again in 1997.

But Woods was also playing as he had the previous year. And over the last months of the 1996 season, no one, not even Lehman, had played as well as Tiger Woods.

In round three, it first seemed as if Woods would have to settle for a top-five finish and concede the tournament to leader Lehman. He was down by four shots as he approached the 15th hole.

All he did then was finish with four birdies, good enough to pull into a tie with Lehman. When the fourth round was rained out the following day, tournament officials decided to hold a sudden death playoff between Woods and Lehman to decide the championship.

In his second playoff test, Woods set out to prove that his earlier win over Davis Love III in a similar situation was no fluke.

The playoff started — and ended — on the par-3 7th hole. Lehman's tee shot landed in the water to the left of the green. Woods's ball rolled to within a foot of the cup. He tapped in to win.

Yet not even Woods could win every week. He finished eighteenth at the Phoenix Open in his next tournament, and when he started the Pebble Beach National Pro-Am with rounds of 70 and 72, there were plenty of whispers that Woods's remarkable run was over.

Pebble Beach is a tough and demanding course. Dramatically set along the ocean in Pebble Beach, California, the layout was fraught with winds that often played havoc with the best players. Tiger barely made the cut. Winning the tournament seemed out of the question.

It was, for anyone but Woods. He made some adjustments in his swing and shot a 63 in round three, only one shot off the course record. Still, he trailed leader Mark O'Meara by five shots entering the final round.

It appeared as if O'Meara's lead would hold. By the 16th hole, Woods still trailed by two shots.

He closed to within one with a birdie. Then O'Meara, playing just behind Woods, also birdied the hole to restore his two-stroke lead. Both men then birdied 17. As Woods teed off on the par-5 18th, he still trailed by two.

He needed either an eagle or a total collapse by O'Meara in order to win. Neither seemed likely.

But Woods was able to do something no other golfer in the game could accomplish with as much consistency as he did. On 18 he hit two towering drives. The second landed on the green. An eagle, and a possible tie for the lead, lay forty feet away.

He lined up the putt carefully and rolled it toward the hole. It drifted right and stopped a few feet away. He tapped in for a birdie.

Woods then watched as O'Meara parred the hole to win by one. Woods had lost, but only by a stroke in one of the greatest comebacks in the history of the game. His final two rounds of 63 and 64 were the best closing rounds in the history of the tournament.

After Pebble Beach, Woods began to look ahead to the Masters Tournament, scheduled to begin on

Thursday, April 10. Ever since he was a child he had imagined himself winning the tournament, beating Jack Nicklaus or some other famous golfer on the back nine of the final round to win the coveted green jacket awarded to the tourney winner.

The tournament was important to Woods for more than its status as the first "major" event of his professional career. As part African-American, he was well aware of the tournament's larger significance. He wanted to win, badly.

He played in only three tournaments over the ensuing three months, finishing twentieth, ninth, and thirty-first. Most of his time was spent on the practice green, dreaming of the course in Augusta, Georgia. He had videotaped a number of previous Masters Tournaments, and he watched as the best golfers in the world struggled to master the course.

Of the four major championships, only the Masters is played on the same course year after year. That's part of the reason why the Masters is held in such esteem by so many golfers and golf fans. They can look at almost any spot on the course and recall what happened there in the past. In the 1996 Masters, golfer Greg Norman, who had already come close to winning the tournament several times, blew a huge lead on the final round to lose in one of the biggest collapses in the history of the PGA.

That's what the Augusta National course did to golfers. It looked deceptively easy to play, yet required a well-rounded, balanced game few golfers had. And entrants weren't just competing against each other when they played the Masters. They were competing against history. In the course clubhouse, there is even a special lounge that only former winners of the tournament are allowed to enter.

Woods was not alone with his obsession over the tournament. The press and his fellow golfers picked up on his fixation. Jack Nicklaus, who won the coveted jacket a record six times, thought Woods's game was perfect for the course. He boldly predicted a Woods win, and went even further when he added, "Before it's all over, he should win at least ten of these."

Others were not so sure. Woods's nondescript play in the weeks preceding the Masters left many with the feeling he was struggling with his game. Besides, in his two previous appearances in the tournament as an amateur, including the 1996 tournament,

Woods had struggled. While there was no doubt his game had improved dramatically since then — particularly in his iron play, which was critical to success at the Masters — there was no way to know how much it had improved until Woods began playing.

The tournament began on Thursday, April 10. As usual, Woods began slowly.

With the gallery already surrounding the entire first hole, his tee shot went astray and he struggled to make a bogey. Throughout the front nine, his driver continued to betray him, as three more times he found himself preparing to take his second shot from amid the trees that framed nearly every hole. He bogeyed three more times to finish the first nine holes with a 4-over-par 40.

Many thought his tournament was over. No one had ever won the Masters playing so poorly on the first nine holes.

As Tiger approached the 10th hole to begin the back nine, he tried to figure out what he was doing wrong. So far, his second shots had saved him. His tee shots were the trouble.

Then suddenly he knew. He had to back off on his tee shots a little and make sure he played with control.

He had simply been taking the club too far back on his backswing. If he could get his first shot down, he thought, the rest of his game appeared to be in place.

It was like turning on a light switch. He hit a perfect drive on 10 and birdied the hole easily. He parred 11 and on 12 made a short chip to the hole. He followed with a two-putt birdie on 13, parred 14, then made a stunning eagle on 15 after knocking his second shot, a wedge, to within four feet of the hole. He birdied the rest of the round, and finished the back nine with a remarkable 30, finishing the day with a 2-under-par 70. At the end of the day he was only three shots behind leader John Huston, who himself had shot a 31 on the final nine holes.

But now Tiger had everyone's attention. On the second day of the tournament, he started in the second-to-the-last twosome, just in front of Huston. All day long, the leader would have Woods's score staring back at him on the leader board.

Woods played well from the beginning. Now that he had gained control of his tee shots, he cut loose, and started driving the ball his accustomed 300-plus yards down the middle of the fairway. He shot a 34 on the front nine. Meanwhile, Huston hung on.

Woods broke Huston on the 13th hole. After a perfect drive on the par 5, he smacked an eight-iron to within twenty feet of the pin, answering any lingering questions about his iron play. Then he drilled a twenty-foot putt for an eagle.

The gallery went nuts. "You the man!" replaced "Shhh!" as the most popular phrase on the golf course.

Huston capsized in Woods's wake. It took him ten agonizing strokes to do what Woods had accomplished in three. His tournament was over. Now the name "Woods" was atop the leader board.

He continued his scorching performance for the rest of the round, and finished with a 66. Halfway through the Masters, he led Colin Montgomerie by three.

Woods oozed confidence when he met with the press after the round. "This is what I came here to do," he said. "I'm looking forward to enjoying the round with Colin."

When asked if the huge crowd following him caused him any problems, Woods just laughed and quipped, "They're stopping a couple of shots," in reference to a shot or two he had bounced off the crowd. "They're rooting me on. That's kind of neat."

On Saturday, every player in the field began their round knowing Woods was on a roll. To remain in contention they would have to play their best possible golf.

No one did. The entire field played as if they were all looking over their shoulder, wondering what Woods was going to do. Meanwhile, he was the only player on the course who was unaffected by the pressure. He might as well have been back at Heartwell, shooting for "Tiger par" again.

He birdied four of the nine holes on the front nine and three more on the back, never came close to a bogey, and shot a 65. His lead rocketed to nine strokes. He was already 15 under par, 13-under for the last two days alone. After the round, the other pros were incredulous.

"I might have a chance," said one of his opponents in the final round, "if I make five or six birdies on the first two or three holes." That utter impossibility said it all.

In the final round, Woods's only competition was history and himself. He was on pace to set a record low score for the tournament and one of the lowest scores in the history of professional golf. His father warned him before he started that "this will be the most difficult round of your life." Woods knew better than to try to play it safe or take unnecessary chances, either of which might cause him to lose his swing and allow someone else to get back in contention.

As Tiger made his way to the first tee, Lee Elder spoke his few private words of wisdom before stepping back to let the youngster begin his final round. Woods was forced to wait for a moment as security made a path through the growing crowd, then teed up the ball. It went long and deep down the fairway, riding a wave of noise pouring from the throats of everyone in the gallery.

For the fourth round, virtually every person on the golf course but the players themselves followed Woods from hole to hole, roaring with pleasure at his every move. Woods nailed a birdie on the 2nd hole, then bogeyed 5 and 7 before birdieing 8 and making the turn at even par.

The last nine holes weren't a golf tournament, but a coronation. Woods birdied 11, 13, and 14 to effectively end any lingering possibility of a collapse. As other golfers finished their final round at the 18th green, many decided to stay, turning from player to spectator.

On the par-3 16th, Woods drove to the green and hit a difficult curving putt to save par. On 17, he parred again.

Only one hole remained between Tiger Woods and the future of the game. Probably the largest, most varied gallery in the history of golf at that time surrounded the entire hole, in some places thirty people deep or more. Fans strained to see past one another, and fathers lifted their sons and daughters to their shoulders. Black and white faces all looked at Woods and saw a hero they felt they could claim as their own.

Woods teed off, and for the first time in three days, he hit a bad shot that hooked far left. But the crowd was with him. A fan who later certainly bragged of it was struck by the ball before it came to rest.

Woods decided to hit a wedge to the green, and looked for his caddie. But Fluff Cowan was caught in the mob, surrounded by well-wishers. Tiger was finally forced to jump up and down, trying to look over the crowd and calling out "Fluff!" at the peak of each leap.

The joyous crowd picked up on Woods's lead and began chanting Fluff's name in unison. The grinning, mustachioed bear of a man finally emerged and handed Woods his wedge. All Tiger could do was smile.

The wedge shot made the green. The two men then walked together to the final hole.

Surrounded by sudden silence, Woods putted the ball toward the hole for a final birdie. He missed, and the ball stopped rolling five feet from the cup. Woods grimaced, but a moment later tapped in the short putt. He had won.

Suddenly, the green became like center stage after a grand dramatic performance. The crowd stood and cheered and clapped and refused to stop. Woods threw an uppercut punch in celebration, as if providing a final knockout blow. He was, after all, now golf's undisputed champion.

He then turned to Fluff and the two men embraced, a white caddy and a black golfer. Then Tiger's father and mother emerged from the crowd, and Woods embraced them, too, holding on to his father for a full twenty seconds, lingering for a moment on the site of his greatest achievement, a place that in every Masters Tournament played in the future, people will turn to and say, "That's where Tiger Woods was when he won." Security made a path through the crowd, and Woods began the slow walk to the ceremony where he would receive his green jacket.

His performance was mind-boggling. His 18-under-par 270 was a course record, bettering the scores made by Ray Floyd in 1971 and Jack Nicklaus in 1965. For the tournament, he played the back nine in a record 16 under par, breaking a record previously held by Arnold Palmer by four shots. He defeated the best golfers in the world by an amazing twelve shots, the largest margin of victory in any major tournament ever. He was the youngest winner of a major, and the first African-American to win.

Lee Elder emerged from the crowd and gave Tiger a hug as well. There were tears in the eyes of both men. "Thanks for making this possible," whispered Tiger.

Then 1996 Masters champion Nick Faldo slipped the traditional green jacket over Woods's shoulders. Tiger accepted with a wide, beaming smile. After all, he had spent the last twenty years making sure it would be a perfect fit.

"I've always dreamed of coming up eighteen and winning," said Woods afterward. "But I never thought this far through the ceremony."

Then he paused and said, "I wasn't the pioneer. Charlie Sifford, Lee Elder, Ted Rhodes, those are the guys who paved the way. All night I was thinking about them, what they've done for me and the game of golf. Coming up eighteen, I said a little prayer of thanks to those guys. Those guys are the ones that did it.

"I think winning here is going to do a lot for the game of golf," he added. "With my age and influence on the game, more young people will start to play.

"Now kids will think 'Golf is cool.'"

Chapter Eleven:
1997–2000

Mr. Major

For most professional golfers, such an imposing victory in such an important tournament would be the highlight of their careers. But Woods soon gave notice that he considered his Masters win just the beginning. He wasn't satisfied.

Woods's goal remained to "win every time I play." But even though he followed his Masters win with a victory in the next tournament he played in, the Byron Nelson Classic, he slumped in the months following that win.

Part of the reason was Woods's newfound fame. After the Masters, observers looked for him to be as dominant every time he stepped onto a golf course. Expectations were raised dramatically. And his victory suddenly made him one of the most recognizable people in the world. Everywhere he went he was swamped with attention.

Woods struggled with maintaining his focus. He played another thirteen tournaments after the Nelson Classic, and though he won one, the Western Open, he was inconsistent in the others and often finished far back in the pack. In one tournament, the Canadian Open, he even missed the cut. People started to whisper that while Woods was undoubtedly a very good golfer and would have a fine career, success had come too early and too easily for him. They wondered whether he would ever fulfill his apparently limitless potential.

Woods's poor performance in the Canadian Open caused him to reassess both his golf game and his approach to fame. One day he sat down with coach Butch Harmon and watched his Masters victory on videotape.

Woods didn't like what he saw. Although he'd played well, he noticed that his swing was too inconsistent, saying later, "To play consistently from the positions my swing was in was going to be very difficult." His putting had also become very streaky, a problem he later admitted was because, with all the new demands on his time, he didn't have enough time to practice.

He still wanted to win every time he played. In order to reach that goal, he decided to change everything, both on and off the golf course.

Few other golfers would have risked changing a style that had worked so well, but his inability to remain satisfied is one of the things that makes Woods different from other athletes. He pared back on his outside activities and went to work with Harmon.

They spent hours on the practice range retooling his swing, particularly his backswing, which they shortened up to give him more control without sacrificing his prodigious length off the tee. He didn't stop competing or trying to win tournaments, but he was more focused on his technique.

Woods also worked on his fitness level, increasing his weight work and strength to create, as Harmon put it, "a very stable base, which makes it easier for him to repeat his swing." He added twenty pounds of muscle to his frame.

Woods and Harmon weren't discouraged when he finished the 1997 tour season with three more lackluster finishes. They knew it would take a while before their results began showing up on the golf course.

He began the 1998 season with an encouraging second-place finish in the Mercedes Championships. In the tournaments that followed, he began to play more consistently. But victory remained elusive. He finished eighth in the Masters, and his only victory of the season came in the Bell South Classic in May. Although Woods usually finished in the top ten and ended the year fourth on the money list with just under two million dollars earned in tournament play, the future of the game now seemed to rest in the hands of other young players, like David Duval, South African Ernie Els, and Spanish teenage sensation Sergio Garcia.

But Woods was undeterred and continued to retool his game. He even let go caddie Fluff Cowan and hired veteran Steve Williams, who had an impeccable reputation for his ability to read greens and give unsparing advice on course management.

Despite opening the 1999 season with three more disappointing finishes, including a tie for 18th place at the Masters, Woods remained confident. Although it wasn't yet showing up in his scores on the golf course, each week he felt more comfortable with his new swing. Now Woods's challenge became to adapt the way he played and managed the course to his new set of abilities. He continued to work on his putting and spent an equal amount of time on his wedge play. He didn't want his game to have any weaknesses. No matter what course he was playing or what situation he found himself in, he wanted to be sure he could make the shot he needed to make.

His progress became apparent in Jack Nicklaus's tough Memorial Tournament in early June, when he blew away the field with a 15-under 273, only his second victory since July of 1997. Two weeks later he finished third in the U.S. Open, then won the Western Open and finished seventh in the British Open. It was an impressive string of performances in a series of tournaments played under conditions that varied widely from one to another.

Woods knew that the upcoming 1999 PGA Championship at the Medinah Country Club would provide a big test for his new game. But not even Woods could imagine just how demanding it would be.

Playing flawlessly, he surged to the lead in the first three rounds and entered the final round tied with

Mike Weir and two shots ahead of Garcia. After birdieing four of the first 11 holes, Woods's lead ballooned to five strokes over Garcia, and Weir fell back even further.

Then Woods suffered a rare slip, losing four shots to par over the next five holes to give Garcia a chance. It didn't help that the crowd had warmed to the effervescent young Spaniard and was cheering him the way it had cheered Woods two years earlier at the Masters.

As Woods said later, "When I got to seventeen I knew I would have to play the best two holes of my life." All his hard work over the previous two years would be put to the test.

The 17th hole at Medinah is treacherous. Although it is only 212 yards long, the golfer has to hit downhill over a water hazard to a small green backed by thick rough.

Woods pulled out a six-iron and went for the hole, hoping to stop his shot on the green. He hit the ball well, but with too much strength. The shot sailed over the green and landed in the rough.

He had a poor lie and had to stand awkwardly over the ball as he considered his chip shot. A year or two before, Woods's play around the green had been the weakest part of his game. But his recent improvement had been dramatic.

Woods took a deep breath, drew the club back slowly, and chopped at the ball. It hopped up into the air and landed on the green, stopping eight feet above the cup, a good but not great shot. But more important, it gave him a chance.

Now he stood over the ball and considered the putt. During his two-year "slump," such shots were precisely those that Woods had failed to make at critical moments.

Yet now his stroke was certain and sure. He confidently rolled the ball into the cup to save par, then played 18 perfectly to secure his second victory in a major championship.

"I'm learning how to play the game," he told reporters in a press conference after the tournament. "I've learned more shots, and it's just getting better." Then he laughed and added, "I'm not that old. I'm not over the hill yet."

Over the next few months, he proved that was the case. Beginning with the World Series of Golf in late August, he won four consecutive tournaments and played a key role in the United States' stirring comeback victory over Europe in the 1999 Ryder Cup. By the end of the year every golfer in the world was wondering just how good Tiger Woods had become.

In the first half of the 2000 PGA Tour, Woods demonstrated that there were no apparent limits to his talent. He won the first two tournaments that he competed in and three of the first five before "slumping" in the Players Championship and the Masters, finishing second and fifth, respectively. But it didn't take Woods long to get back on track.

In late June he ran away with the U.S. Open at the fabled seaside Pebble Beach Golf Links in California. While other players struggled with the always-tough course — where the conditions were made even more difficult by wind, rain, and fog —Woods played the course as if impervious to the weather. He won the tournament with a score of 12-under par, an incredible 15 shots ahead of second-place finisher Ernie Els. Els spoke for the entire field after the tournament when he said of Woods's performance, "My words probably can't describe it, so I'm not even going to try."

A month later, at the British Open played at the legendary St. Andrews Golf Club in Scotland, Woods again left the opposition speechless. He scorched the course and left the world's greatest golfers in his wake, finishing 19-under par and eight shots ahead of Els, the largest margin of victory in the tournament in 87 years. Veteran Tom Watson called the performance "supernatural" and added, "He has raised the bar to a level only he can jump."

The victory put Tiger on course to tie a PGA record that many thought was unattainable. In 1953, golfing legend Ben Hogan won three consecutive majors, the only time any golfer has done so. With a victory in the PGA at Valhalla in Louisville, Kentucky, Woods could match Hogan's record.

For the first two days of the tournament he was paired with Jack Nicklaus, whose records Woods had once posted on his bedroom wall. As thousands followed the two golfers around the course over the first two days of the tournament, they witnessed the passing of the baton from Nicklaus, who many had once considered the greatest golfer in history, to Woods, who now seemed to hold that title. At the end of the first two rounds, Woods led the tournament by a shot with a score of 11-under, causing Nicklaus to comment wistfully, "He's better now than I ever was."

After shooting a 70 in the third round, Woods seemed poised to walk away with the tournament on the final day. He led challenger Bob May, who had never won a PGA tournament, by a single stroke.

But on the front nine of the final round, for seemingly the first time in months, Woods stumbled. On the second hole, he collected a bogey while May birdied to take the lead. They ended the front nine tied, each at 13-under par.

What followed was perhaps the most exciting finish in golf history. Woods and May matched each other shot for spectacular shot. But as the two players sat on the green of the 15th hole, May led by a stroke and seemed poised to put the tournament away.

Woods needed to sink a 15-foot putt just to make par, while May had an easy four-footer for a birdie. Woods shot first.

"I knew if I made mine, it would make his a little longer," said Woods later. He settled over the ball, absolutely still, and drained the long putt to save par.

As Woods had hoped, that put the pressure on May. For the first time all day, he allowed the pressure to affect him and missed the easy putt. The two players were tied.

They were still tied at the 18th hole. Then both players made mistakes. May left his approach shot nearly 100 feet from the hole. Woods was closer, some 35 feet away, but with a difficult ridge still to negotiate on the green.

May shot first and left his putt 15 feet from the hole. Then Woods putted, rolling the ball up the ridge, 30 degrees away from the hole, then watched it curl down and back.

It was a spectacular shot, but still six feet short.

It was a difficult putt, but May read it perfectly. The ball first broke left, then right, then dropped in the cup on its last revolution. Now Woods needed to hole out to force a tie.

Like a boxer refusing to fall, Woods nailed the putt. The two players shook hands and walked to the 16th hole to begin their three-hole playoff. Each had completed the final nine holes 5-under par.

Now both players showed the effects of the long tournament, as each began to struggle. But on 16

Woods retained his composure long enough to record a birdie, while May scrambled to make par. Neither man shot well on the next two holes, but when Woods blasted out of a sand trap on 18 to within two feet of the hole, and May missed a long putt, Woods knew he had it. He tapped in for the win.

He had tied Hogan's record! Even more incredible was the fact that in each of his three consecutive major victories, Woods had set a new scoring record.

"This was one of the best duels in the game," Woods said later. "One memorable battle. We never backed off. We went birdie for birdie, shot for shot. It was a very special day." For Tiger Woods, age 25 and already the greatest player the game has ever known, every time he walks on the golf course is already a very special day.

MATT CHRISTOPHER

The #1 Sports Series for Kids

Read them all!

All available in paperback from Little, Brown and Company

Matt Christopher

Terrell Davis	*Lisa Leslie*
John Elway	*Tara Lipinski*
Julie Foudy	*Mark McGwire*
Wayne Gretzky	*Greg Maddux*
Ken Griffey Jr.	*Hakeem Olajuwon*
Mia Hamm	*Briana Scurry*
Grant Hill	*Sammy Sosa*
Derek Jeter	*Tiger Woods*
Randy Johnson	*Steve Young*
Michael Jordan	